THE BEST
OF THE MAJOR

by Galen Winter

COUNTRYSPORT PRESS
CAMDEN, MAINE

OTHER BOOKS BY GALEN WINTER

Summer of '38

Legendary Northwoods Animals

*Backlash—a compendium of lore and lies (mostly lies)
concerning hunting, fishing and the out-of-doors*

500 Wisconsin Fish and Game Recipes

Text © 2002 by Galen Winter
Cover illustration © 2002 by Loren Smith

Jacket design by Jan Njaa
Interior design by Park Morrison
Printed by Versa Press Inc., East Peoria, IL

5   4   3   2   1

ISBN 0-89272-540-0

Library of Congress Control Number: 2002108133

COUNTRYSPORT PRESS
Camden, Maine

For orders and catalog information, call 800-685-7962
or visit www.downeastbooks.com

This book is dedicated to
my hunting and fishing *compadres*—
Steve and Mike and Doug
and Jim and Tom and Paul

CONTENTS

PREFACE

During the fall of 1987, I was in a wild part of Wood County in Wisconsin, engaged in the woodcock and ruffed-grouse hunt that is, every year, undertaken by a group of outdoor writers. Steve Smith was there. He is a sportswriter, an author, and an editor.

Steve confessed he was planning to publish a magazine dedicated to hunting dogs and shotgunning. He was going to call it *Shooting Sportsman.* That magazine, he told me, might have use for a column chronicling the hunting exploits of a retired army officer, an avid shotgunner, and a world traveler. Steve further explained that the protagonist would be one man, not three.

That's how I met Major Nathaniel Peabody, USA (ret.).

Beyond the facts that he was retired and an accomplished bird hunter, I knew nothing about him. Over the ensuing months and years, as I became acquainted with him, I grew to both know and appreciate the old gentleman.

The Major's a cynic, I suppose.

He has no confidence in politicians. He presumes all of their actions are taken for the sole purpose of securing reelection and, thus, avoiding honest labor.

He believes that those who profess great social conscience and those who support organizations promising to improve humanity, would avoid the black plague.

If anyone, other than a trusted friend, says he is going to do something nice for you, the Major's advice is: Keep your hand on your wallet, get your back to the wall, and carefully, but quickly, edge toward the nearest exit.

The Major questions the motives of anyone who attempts to raise money by public subscription. He will admit that some of them, like Ducks Unlimited, Trout Unlimited, and The Nature Conservancy, do good work. The stated objectives of many of the others, he says, are praiseworthy beyond reproach but mask their real purpose, which is to trap the unwary into providing a substantial salary for the fundraiser.

Moreover, if Major Peabody's opinion is solicited, he will not be intimidated by what is known as the "politically correct." Against his better judgment, the Major may attend an afternoon social gathering. Though he may be a minority of one, his answers to questions concerning gun-control legislation will not be bland or temporizing. They will probably come as a terrible shock to those present.

Putting it another way, Major Nathaniel Peabody, USA (ret.) has never been housebroken.

His extreme independence makes the Major popular in some circles and quite unpopular in others. However, the matters that are important to the Major do not include a longing for popularity, involvement with any of the temporary fads of society, or conformity with the politically correct.

Shooting over an English setter on an abandoned Georgia farm, watching a November sunrise from a Manitoba duck blind, calling Argentine geese into a decoy set spread out on a Patagonia plain, enjoying single-malt Scotch whisky and a Dominican Republic cigar after a meal of grouse, cooked in an iron skillet over a campfire—these are the pursuits that attract the Major.

They do more than merely attract him. They demand the Major. And he happily answers the call. Our lives are different. We hear calls. We think about answering them.

When that black shadow taps us on the shoulder and says, "You're next, friend," almost all of us will say: "Hey. Wait a minute. I wasn't expecting this just now. There are some things I've been planning to do, but I simply haven't had the time . . . you know. How about coming back in a year?"

And the shadow will repeat: "You're next, friend."

The Major would make an entirely different comment. I wish I were Major Nathaniel Peabody.

GALEN WINTER
Shawano, Wisconsin

FOREWORD

I should confess from the outset: I don't know a lot about Galen Winter. In the almost nine years I've edited *Shooting Sportsman*, he's the only masthead editor—and there are fifteen—whom I've never met. I'm not sure whether it has been fate or design, but we've managed to avoid each other, which perhaps explains why our relationship remains solid after all this time.

Most of what I do know about Galen I've cobbled together through phone conversations and correspondence. I know, for example, that Galen was once a lawyer but that he gave it up to spend more time hunting and fishing. I like that. I also know he's a man who enjoys traveling, for his letters and postcards are as likely to arrive from Wisconsin or Florida as they are from Central or South America. I prefer to think of Galen as an "international man of mystery," one who's blessed with an innate sense of humor. Kind of an F. Lee Bailey meets Austin Powers, minus the cool threads.

Another thing I know is that Galen can write . . . and write well. Each time I begin editing a new issue of *Shooting Sportsman*, I go to his column first, not only because it lets me start off with a good chuckle but because I seldom have to do much work to it. That he writes in a genre many say is the toughest—humor—is an added testament to his talent.

The proof of Galen's success is his longevity with the magazine. As I write this, *SSM* is in its fourteenth year and, according to Galen, he is "the only writer who has conned the management into publishing an article in every one of the issues since its inception."

More proof comes from reader letters and from comments made at sporting shows. "The Major is my favorite part of the magazine" is an oft-heard testimonial. "I always turn to the back page first." One fellow even claimed to customarily read Galen's column to his wife in bed. "Major" praise, indeed.

Before signing on with *SSM*, I worked at *Outdoor Life* magazine, where one of my jobs was editing Pat McManus's "The Last Laugh." I don't think many would disagree that Pat is the dean of outdoor humor writing, but neither would they deny that Pat and Galen have a lot in common. Both are talented wordsmiths and, though each has a unique style and method of story-crafting, the results are always the same: They make you laugh. One difference is that what Pat often achieves with slapstick, Galen does with dry wit, making Galen, in my mind, "the thinking man's McManus."

Sometimes the humor is so cerebral it escapes me—and the author himself. I remember the time Galen called in a panic, having discovered he'd been the unwitting participant in a joke. It seems he'd had a confidante with whom he had often discussed column ideas. At one point the friend had suggested a name for the firm that Major Peabody's young lawyer works for: Smythe, Hauser, Ingalls & Tauchen. Galen had liked it. Only after a reader pointed out the offensive acronym did Galen realize he'd been had—and on further reflection more than once. He was contrite and apologetic . . . and "Ingalls" began spelling his name with an "E."

In addition to admiring his ethics, I also appreciate Galen's adherence to deadlines. In the past nine years he has never missed one. The only time he came close, he included a two-page letter explaining his tardiness—a letter that must have taken as long to write as the column itself. In it he described a deer hunt on which he'd spent the day in a Wisconsin tree stand. During a particularly slow time he'd penned the column, then rolled up the pages and "laid them on the shelf next to the candy bars, coffee, paperback copy of *Extraordinary Popular Delusions and Madness of Crowds*, cigars, and matches."

Ten minutes before dark he had heard noises behind him, and as he slowly pivoted he'd inadvertently knocked the manuscript to the ground. It turned out the noises were being made by a fox, which, unbelievably, had proceeded to grab the manuscript and spirit it away to his den.

"Magpies, I am told, are fascinated by bright and shining things," wrote Galen. "They collect such objects and hoard them in their nests. (I once had a wife who was the same way.) This felonious fox, it seems to me, must have had a penchant for stealing paper. Perhaps he used it to insulate his lair."

By then it had become dark, but Galen had courageously approached the den, reached in, felt his manuscript and, following a tug of war with the fox, managed to pull the pages out. He then had promptly returned to camp, whereupon he'd related his story to his friends.

"I was met with guffaws and repeated direct accusations of sham and deception. I'm afraid the words 'liar' and 'damned liar' were used. And when I took the papers from my hunting coat to defend my truthful reputation and show them positive proof of my story, to my chagrin I held in my hand only some rolled-up pages of the *Green Bay Press-Gazette*. The fox still had the manuscript.

"I had to admit it. I didn't know my mss. from a scroll in the ground."

Obviously, Galen is not one for simple explanations. Consider the time a reader took him to task for spelling Irish whiskey without an "e." His response, in part, read: "It has been my position that 'whisky' is the spelling of the ambrosia—Scotch whisky. 'Whiskey' is the spelling of product made in the United States—usually with a corn base. U.S. distillers used to keep it straight, but in the last twenty or so years, they call some of their stuff 'whisky.' The Canadians tend to refer to their booze as 'whisky,' and the Irish, well . . .

". . . David Duffey has been the editor of the dog sections of various magazines and claims to be thoroughly Irish. When we get together, the subject of 'whisky/whiskey' comes up and is the focus of erudite discussion—usually continuing into the wee hours of the morning. I'm sure we have unsnarled that particular philological mess on a number of occasions.

"Unfortunately, due to peculiar qualities of Jamiesons, Maker's Mark, and The Glenlivet, on the following day we are quite unable to recall the conclusions, and our notes are illegible—conditions we both blame on my wife. However, we will persevere, and when our tract is ready for publication in the appropriate journals, a copy will be forwarded to you."

Another time, in answer to a question regarding the origin of the word "pheasant," he wrote: "The Rioni River flows down the Caucusus and enters the Black Sea. During the olden days when the Greeks were big shots, the river was known as the Phasis. The

Greeks called the bird that was common to the area, the *phásiánós*—in Latin, *phásiánus,* in Anglo Norman, *fesaunt,* and in English, pheasant.

"Incidentally, the word 'partridge' originally came into the English language as 'patriarch,' which came from the Greek word *'perdix.'* In ancient Greece, *'perdix'* meant 'one who expels wind.' From this I conclude that the biologist who gave the bird its Latin designation of *Perdix perdix* either stuttered or was particularly flatulent."

And so it goes. Every two months I receive another installment of "The Major"—and another window onto the man who created the unconventional curmudgeon we all wish we knew . . . and had along at boring parties when confronted by anti-hunting types in comfortable shoes. Luckily, it appears that Galen will be around for a while. In a recent correspondence on death and dying he confided:

"Except for the feeling of excruciating pain whenever I hear a saxophone, I am ignorant in matters musical—and this includes the harp. I am tone deaf. My attempts at singing have made competent musicians grimace and openly weep.

"Were I allowed in heaven, I could neither play the harp nor join the heavenly choir without profoundly disrupting the perfect harmony of the place. And I suspect some of the angels might object to my cigars and single-malt Scotch whisky.

"My presence would, I fear, tempt those in the angelic choir (who were within hearing range) to resort to language not commonly associated with the cherubim. It would certainly cause them to petition a higher authority for my removal from the Elysian fields.

"No, they'll never let me in up there.

"On the other hand, the people who know about such things assure me I won't go to hell. This comes as an acute disappointment to me because I had so looked forward to meeting you during my afterlife.

"Because I was an attorney, the devil has barred me from Hades. He claims there are too many lawyers down there already. He says they are a disagreeable lot, spending all their time questioning his jurisdiction, disputing his authority, and in general raising hell. He'll have no more of them.

"It looks as if I'm going to live forever."

On behalf of thinking sportsmen everywhere, I certainly hope so. I don't know what we'd do without him.

RALPH P. STUART
Editor in Chief
Shooting Sportsman

The devil is clever
Not because he is the devil,
But because he is old.

—SPANISH PROVERB

MAJOR
NATHANIEL PEABODY,
USA (RET.)

FOLLOWING A WELL-ESTABLISHED FAMILY tradition William Henry Peabody served with distinction in the United States diplomatic corps. While attached to the embassy in Bogota in the Republic of Colombia, he met, fell in love with, and married the daughter of a wealthy Peruvian landowner who had been temporarily exiled from his own country as a result of one of its 1920s revolutions.

William Henry's wife's family name, Palma, was as old and distinguished in Peru as is the name Peabody in the United States. Their union produced a son, Nathaniel Alberto Peabody Palma.

During its more than three-and-a-half centuries in the New World, the Peabody family seldom produced a black sheep. Unquestionably, William Henry and Maria Teresa produced one.

Born in Bogota, Nathaniel spent his early years in the capital cities of various Latin American republics. This accounts for his fluency in the Spanish language, his intimate knowledge of Latin culture, and his inborn distrust of and antagonism toward all forms of authority, especially governmental authority.

When he was a teenager, his escapades were an embarrassment to both his American and Peruvian relatives. Nathaniel was, therefore, banished to the United States, where he received his education in military academies. I say military academ*ies* because he was asked to leave more than one of them.

Though Nathaniel Peabody was uncomfortable in the military ambiance, which he says "is unreasonably obsessed with rules and regulations," in 1943 he decided upon a career in the United States Army. He had an ulterior motive and a plan.

Because of his fluency in the Spanish language (and because of his family connections), Lieutenant Nathaniel Peabody was sent to a Central American embassy, where he served as a military attaché. This made it possible for him to spend considerable amounts of time engaging in his shotgunning avocations. And, as Peabody was well aware, the hunting in Latin America was (and continues to be) excellent.

Promotion came slowly to Peabody due to his lack of West Point credentials and, equally, to his unfortunate tendency to be coolly insubordinate to his superiors but warmly familiar with their wives. After thirty years of service, he retired with the rank of Major.

Major Peabody's army retirement pay doesn't begin to cover his living expenses. He treats money with an indifference approaching contempt. Money is only a convenience, useful to provide for the Major's own immediate needs. As quickly as he gets his hands on it, he spends it.

And his "immediate needs," which include single-malt Scotch

whisky and imported cigars, are largely limited to expenditures associated with bird hunting. His monthly income is, certainly, not modest. It would provide you or me with a comfortable lifestyle. But Major Nathaniel Peabody, USA (ret.) is always without funds at the end of the month.

William Henry Peabody was painfully aware of his son's profligate ways. I know whereof I speak. William Henry, himself, often emphasized the matter when we discussed the terms of the spendthrift trust segment of the Peabody estate plan.

I am a junior partner in the Philadelphia law firm of Smythe, Hauser, Engels & Tauchen. My area of specialization is estate planning. I drafted the Peabody family spendthrift trust document. Its terms, to use the Major's phrase, are tighter than the bark on a paper birch tree. No pledging. No alienation of any sort. And no loopholes.

By background and experience, I had little in common with Major Peabody. I'm not an outdoors type. I don't hunt. Frankly, I'm afraid of wild animals—especially bears. I don't like dogs. They are smelly and, at times, they growl at me for no apparent reason. I don't smoke. Occasionally, I take wine at dinner and a highball or two at a social event. Classical music and the opera soothe my soul.

Major Peabody has no time for classical music or the opera. It isn't that he's ignorant of them. They just aren't important to him. Scratching a hunting dog's ears soothes the Major

I'm conservative in matters financial. I require the security of a sound investment portfolio and adequate liquid funds. The Major couldn't care less about such things. His assets consist of a few Lefever shotguns, the clothes on his back, the change in his pockets, and other personality, all of which could easily fit into two standard-sized suitcases. None of this bothers him.

It bothers me that it doesn't bother him. And, I'll admit, it also bothered me when, during one or our early meetings, he found occasion to use the objectionable phrase "anally retentive" to describe my lifestyle.

But, in spite of our diametrically opposed views on how one should manage one's life, I've developed a true affection for Major Nathaniel Peabody, USA (ret.). I have the suspicion he has changed me. I know I've developed a taste for scotch.

I can only think of one way in which I may have changed the Major. He no longer uses that objectionable phrase when he refers to me.

DOWN ARGENTINE WAY

WHEN MAJOR NATHANIEL PEABODY, USA (ret.) first appeared at the offices of Smythe, Hauser, Engels & Tauchen, he was unaware of the spendthrift trust established by his then recently deceased father, William Henry Peabody. He expected to receive an outright bequest of a large amount of money. Our senior partner, Robertson Smythe, explained that the Major would receive a check on the first day of each month for the rest of his life—nothing more and nothing less.

The Major's disappointment was such that he violated one of his lifelong rules and hired an attorney, who reviewed the terms of the trust document and advised him it was unbreakable. The Major would simply have to live with it.

Peabody fired the attorney. When he learned I had been assigned the task of administering the trust, he decided to test me and asked for an advance payment. I told him I had to follow the provisions of the trust without deviation whatsoever. I was firm. No advance payment would ever be made.

Major Peabody was not pleased by that announcement, but he soon got his revenge.

Near the end of the following month, I received a telephone

call from Winisk. Winisk is a settlement on the southwest shore of Henry Hudson's Bay. Major Peabody advised me the goose hunting had been superb. He also told me he expected to receive the check due him on the first day of the month. He referred to the provision of the trust document specifically requiring "delivery to Nathaniel Peabody." He emphasized that the terms of the trust demanded there be no deviation whatsoever from its provisions.

"I'll look forward to receiving the check from your very hands, my boy," he said. Then he hung up.

Mr. Smythe laughed. He reminded me that I was the one who drafted the terms of the trust. He told me that Peabody's interpretation of delivery terms was correct and hoped I would have a pleasant trip to the northern part of the province of Ontario.

And on the first day of virtually every month thereafter, I have personally handed the Major his trust remittance. I believe Major Peabody goes out of his way to be in some faraway place at the end of each month. My passport is now filled with stamps.

The following incident is typical.

The intercom buzzed, and my secretary told me I had a collect call from a place called Llao Llao. Major Peabody had not been in his Philadelphia apartment for over a week. I was sure the call was from him.

Yes, he was alive and well. The end of the month was approaching and I knew he must be without funds. And I knew he would ask me to personally hand him his check wherever Llao Llao might be.

Three days later, I arrived in Bariloche on the Aerolineas Argentina flight from Buenos Aires. Bariloche is on the northern side of the Patagonia, on the Andean edge of Argentina and quite near the border with Chile. Its airport is the closest one to Llao Llao.

When Butch Cassidy and the Sundance Kid left the United States for a place where the Pinkertons were less active, they came to the northern part of the Patagonia. It looks a lot like the landscape of Montana, Wyoming, and Utah. It was in Patagonia that the local cattle barons hired these two accomplished rustlers and robbers of banks and trains to protect their herds from the depredations of Argentine bandits. It was a lot like hiring an automobile thief to guard a used-car lot.

Cassidy and the Kid took part of their pay in the form of land located at the eastern end of Lake Nahuel Huapi. This lake is located between the airport and the city of Bariloche. That Butch Cassidy lived near Bariloche is undoubtedly true. I know. I am convinced one of the direct descendants of that renowned bandit operates a taxicab at the Bariloche International Airport. He charged me US$75.00 for the eighteen-mile trip between the airport and the hotel in Llao Llao.

I asked for the Major at the hotel reception desk. The manager gave me a look that seemed to question my character and rather coolly directed me to the hotel terrace. There I found Major Peabody, patiently awaiting my arrival.

"Well, my boy," he greeted me as he rose from a table on the verandah. It overlooked a lake surrounded by green forest and set before a backdrop of snow-covered Andean peaks. "You are timely, as usual. The innkeeper seems to be a bit nervous about the tab I've been running. At least, it's a subject he likes to talk about whenever we meet." I noticed an empty wine glass on the table.

"Come. Sit." I did, feeling like a well-trained hunting dog. "Tell me about your flight."

Before I could react, he answered for me. "A pleasant one. You

fly over the Pampas. An interesting area," and he never returned
to the subject.

"Let me introduce you to a bottle of first-rate Argentine wine,"
he continued, waving to get the attention of a reluctant waiter. "It's
produced in the province of Mendoza, about five hundred miles
north of there. You'll allay the waiter's fears if you pay for it as soon
as he brings it to the table."

Major Peabody's assessment of the wine was entirely accurate.
Halfway through the first glass, he began the kind of hunting dis-
course he truly enjoys—especially when talking to a neophyte like
me.

"You are, of course, acquainted with the Hungarian partridge,"
he said. It was a statement, not a question. As a matter of fact, I was
not acquainted with and have never met even one Hungarian partridge, but I nodded assent anyway. "The people who hang Latin
names on wildlife call it 'Perdix perdix.' That seems to me to be
unnecessarily repetitious, but I won't question their procedures.

"Here in Argentina, there are sixteen different kinds of game
birds carrying the *perdiz* designation in Spanish. They are all
related to the Hun. The *perdiz chica* looks a lot like a hen ruffed
grouse, without the fanned tail. It, too, is a ground bird. It likes
open terrain. There are four varieties of *perdiz chica* to be found in
the provinces of the northern half of the country.

"The *perdiz colorado* has a light, rusty color and is protected.
The *martineta* is a bigger bird. Its feathers are brownish black and
are covered with white speckles. The most curious characteristic of
the *martineta* is a thin crest, like a spit curl. It sits atop the bird's
head, curves forward, and points upward. The *martineta,* as its
name indicates, prefers a more mountainous home.

8

"I've enjoyed excellent *perdiz chica* hunting down here, but were it not for a weakened financial condition, which you are about to cure, I would already have left the hotel for the province of Neuquen. I'm told that state contains a substantial population of both *martineta* and *montaraz*.

"I've already made arrangements to leave for Neuquen before sunrise. Since tomorrow is the first day of the month, it is important that you provide me with the stipulated trust funding at 12:01. I will cover my account with the innkeeper and be on my way before you rise in the morning.

"This suggests we can enjoy each other's company, at least until the new day arrives. I can recommend a local restaurant that serves excellent fried, well-condimented cheese; memorable Argentine beef; and quality wines. It is their custom to remain open until well after midnight. Since there is no single-malt Scotch whisky in Llao Lao, the entire evening won't be very expensive for you."

And the Major was right.

But Argentina can be expensive. On my way back to Philadelphia, I spent an evening in Buenos Aires. I visited another establishment recommended by Major Peabody for a nightcap. It was a strange place located in what could have been a residential section. When my eyes became accustomed to the dark, I saw a lot of attractive women but few men.

One of the young ladies engaged me in conversation and was quite amiable. Intending to order a pair of Benedictines, I had the presence of mind to inquire into the cost. When informed the transaction required an investment of US$25.00, I left the place without further ado.

I've often thought of that experience. I simply can't under-

9

stand how so many unescorted women could afford to spend an evening in such an expensive place.

3

THE BEST LAID SCHEMES

MAJOR PEABODY ARRIVED IN THE GREEN BAY airport on Friday afternoon. He retrieved his baggage from the carousel and left the building. A van, parked in the five-minute zone, awaited him. His hunting companions, an ophthalmologist and an attorney, had been there for half an hour. (It is the policy of the airport police to issue citations only to vehicles that don't carry a Green Bay Packer license plate.)

The attorney tooted the horn to get the Major's attention.

You could tell they were friends of some long standing by the form of their greetings:

"My gawd, how you've aged. You look terrible."

"Have you been disbarred yet, or is the Wisconsin Bar Association Ethics Committee still susceptible to bribery?"

"I'm surprised to see you. I didn't think anyone would be foolish enough to lend you bail money."

"Is there truth to the rumor the Ophthalmologist Society is going to sue Mother Theresa for curing the blind without a license?"

Peabody put his shotgun and gear into the back of the van, already packed with decoys and the other hunters' paraphernalia.

After stopping at a sport shop to buy two more boxes of shells, a Wisconsin hunting license, and a duck stamp for Peabody, the three men drove north to a lake not yet cursed with development. Trees—not cottages crammed cheek to jowl—lined its shores.

The lake was over seven miles long and about three miles wide. In its center, a two-acre island successfully battled the winds and waves that tried to erode it. Reeds and wild rice surrounded the island. A one-room cabin provided shelter for the attorney-owner and his friends.

The three men loaded the motorboat with their equipment and got to the island in time to watch the sun sink into the northwestern horizon and disappear as flights of ducks came to the lake to spend the evening. Soon the Coleman lanterns were lit, the fire in the pot-bellied woodstove heated the cabin, and—since the three friends were civilized sorts—libations made their appearance.

The men sat around the stove and talked until midnight about duck-hunting expeditions past and future, and, especially, about the present one. It would be a short hunt, but it would be a good hunt.

Saturday and Sunday would be devoted to the ducks. Early Monday morning, the doctor and the lawyer would drive back to Green Bay and attend to their professional responsibilities. Major Peabody would return with them and board a flight back to Philadelphia.

All three had great expectations for the morrow. They fell asleep with smiles on their faces. But shortly after they retired, the mercury hunkered down and hid in the bottom of the thermometer. The wind began to blow, and a storm came out of Canada.

They call such a storm an "Alberta Clipper." It races out of the northwest and, with gale-proportion winds, dumps Arctic cold on Wisconsin. Sometimes it carries snow—but not large, soft flakes. A Clipper brings small, hard granules of snow that seem not to fall but fly along, parallel to the ground. The granules sting when they hit the skin.

On Saturday morning, the Arctic wind raced across the lake. It pushed waves ahead of it—waves two-and-a-half to three feet high, waves that sported great whitecaps.

The frigid wind and snow blew directly toward the face of Major Nathaniel Peabody. His optimism of the previous night had undergone a change. It was not a good day to be duck hunting, even though the storm brought flocks of bluebill that had misjudged the length of time they should stay in Canada.

Unflinchingly, the Major looked directly into the icy onslaught and watched as drops of water broke from the whitecaps, fell on his duck skiff, and immediately froze. Then he turned from behind the safety of the cabin's double-paned windows, put another chunk of year-old maple into the potbellied stove, and sat in an overstuffed chair, resting his wool-stockinged feet on a convenient stool.

The hunters were island bound in the midst of a sub-zero, snow-blown gale. The late flight of Canadian bluebill was in progress. But it was impossible to paddle or even motor out to the rice, set the blocks, and hunt or retrieve ducks from the blinds that were strategically constructed around the island. The hunters were in exactly the right place but at exactly the wrong time.

After a while, Major Peabody pulled on his boots and announced to the others: "I believe it would be wise to bring those skiffs and the motorboat a little higher up on the shore. If they are blown away, we'll be marooned here. Frankly, the prospect of being stranded on an island with the two of you is definitely not one calculated to fill me with delight."

The other men advised the Major they had already decided to save two shells for the purpose of committing suicide in the event they had to stay there with him for a protracted period. The Major opened the cabin door and went out into the blustery cold.

Peabody had a hidden agenda. His stated desire to save the boats from loss or damage masked a different purpose. A group of mature willow trees grew on the southeast side of the island. There, he reasoned, the northwest wind might be broken by the trees.

If that were the case, the ducks, having spent a day flying inside a storm, might just drop into that calmer water to rest and fill up with wild rice. Peabody foresaw the potential for a favorable wager. He was sure the attorney would bet he couldn't get a limit of ducks in such weather.

Standing on shore behind the willow trees, the Major watched bluebill come hurtling from the northwest as they rode the storm. But they didn't turn and struggle upwind toward him and the small section of calmer water on the leeward side of the island. They flew on, to the southern edge of the lake.

That shore was bordered by mature evergreens—spruce and hemlock and fir. The thick trees stopped the oncoming wind and created a pocket of calmer water that extended along the entire shoreline. That narrow band of sheltered water was black with ducks. And as the Major watched, even more flights splashed down.

The south shore of the lake was nearly a mile from the island. Not even a duck hunter would be foolhardy enough to get into a boat and face those large, frigid, whitecapped waves. The Major could do no more than watch the ducks and salivate.

Sorely disappointed, Peabody returned to the cabin and again stared out the window, searching for any sign that the storm might abate. There was none. He resumed his seat next to the stove, glowered, and wondered which of his friends was responsible for the vile weather.

The gale continued for all of Saturday. There was more bad news for the Major. That evening, in their boredom, the men were reduced to playing three-handed poker. During a game of seven-card stud, the Major faced an opponent with three aces and two cards of no significance showing. From the way the lawyer bet, it was obvious he had another pair—a full house, aces up.

The Major showed two queens and two nines. But he had another two queens in the hole. Both men bet with enthusiasm, and there were a lot of chips on the table when the final raise was called. The Major's four queens weren't as good as the lawyer's four aces.

The gale continued throughout Sunday. The Major ran out of cigars. That evening he was forced to drink blended Scotch whisky.

After midnight, the storm passed. In the morning, the hunters awoke to more clement weather. The bluebill were still flying, but the men had to leave early. Doc Hitch had an operation at eleven, and the attorney didn't want to be late for a scheduling conference with Judge Luckenbach. Being late for a conference with Judge Luckenbach subjected the offending lawyer to a furious chastisement, phrased in never-to-be-forgotten language.

Peabody had no chance to hunt on Monday morning.

I met the Major at the Philadelphia airport and, after loading his gear into my car, asked him about the hunt. He told me, omitting not even the smallest of his disappointments. He ended up by saying, "I had a marvelous time." Then he smiled and added the cryptic comment: "I don't believe nonhunters would understand."

I wondered what he meant.

4

You Win Some and You Lose Some

BEYOND ACCEPTING THAT MONEY IS AN element essential to his frequent wingshooting forays, Major Nathaniel Peabody, USA. (ret.) treats all matters financial with disdain. His abilities to deal with such affairs are decidedly limited.

And this is why the last generation of Peabodys considered it prudent to devise his portion of their ample estates to a spend-thrift trust. As already noted, I was named trustee, and that position has evolved into one in which I have the unhappy responsibility of supervising the Major's finances—an undertaking similar to that of cleansing the Aegean stables. (And, I sometimes believe, involving a lot of the same kind of material.)

Since the Major's army retirement is sent to me and accompanies his trust remittances when I deliver his checks on the first day of the month, he is, then, wealthy. But on or before the last day of the month he is consistently without funds—flat broke, penniless.

Ever since he learned that people who lend money expect (a) to get paid back, and (b) to receive interest in addition to the principal amount of the loan, the Major has avoided all manner of

17

credit transaction. Assuming his passion for old decoys fits into the "graven image" classification, the only commandment he has not violated since attaining adulthood is: Thou shalt not borrow.

All this means the Major must frequently live by his wits during the last week of the month. If he is not in the field hunting, I am the target of his fund-raising schemes. If he *is* in the field, his associates receive the benefit of his attentions.

So the Major plays poker and is constantly wagering with his hunting buddies. But don't be misled into thinking the Major is a gambler. Oh, no. He never participates in games of chance. Playing poker with him involves little chance. He is almost sure to win, and you are almost sure to lose.

Sane men will not bet with him—regardless of how attractive his proposition may appear. The Major's wagers are carefully crafted to expose him to only a minuscule potential for loss.

The Major will bet that he can throw an unshelled peanut farther than you can. His unshelled peanut will be filled with lead shot. The Major will bet that he can drop a paper match from a height of twenty-four inches and have it land on its edge. He'll fold it in half before he drops it.

You are well advised to never, never, not ever bet with him—especially when it is near the end of the month and, as is customary, he is enjoying a shaky economic condition. When his financial status is at its weakest, the Major's duplicity and chicanery quotients are at their highest. Let me give you an example.

Tom Trowbridge has known the Major for a few years. He and some of his Phoenix pals, who call themselves the Desert Bears, invited the Major to come to Arizona and chase California quail in the Nevada portion of the Sonoran desert. Since the Major had contracted to be in Mexico for a dove hunt on the twenty-fifth of that month, he was happy to spend the prior week hunting with the Bears.

So he arranged for air transportation to Hermosillo with a stopover in Phoenix. He planned to spend the last third of the month first, in the Arizona and later in the Mexican desert. His only connection with places where he could disperse his money would be through a transistor radio. When the day came for him to return to Philadelphia, it would be time for him to receive his first-of-the-month checks, and he would again be financially respectable. But, the best laid schemes o' mice an' men gang aft aglee.

One of the Desert Bears was a banker. On Tuesday evening—the third day of the hunt—the radio reported that the Arizona Banking Commission was in the process of performing an audit of his bank's records.

Major Peabody thought he saw the banker turn a bit green around the gills, but he assigned no special significance to it until the following morning. When the Bears awoke, the banker was not in camp, and one of the vehicles was missing. The Major's plane ticket to Mexico had also mysteriously disappeared.

Peabody found himself in the Arizona bush with a hundred dollars and change. He had two days to drum up enough cash to cover the expense of getting to Hermosillo and the safe haven of his Mexican host's hospitality. The Major stopped hunting quail and started looking for a pigeon.

Peabody knew that Tom Trowbridge was a better-than-average shot, but he was rarely right on target. He seldom really pulverized a clay bird. That evening, when the campfire was glowing, and the cigars and Scotch whisky had been distributed, the Major began his campaign.

He discussed the flight characteristics of quail and the barrel swing of successful quail shooters. Then he laid his trap. He proposed his thesis, to wit: Accomplished hunters like Trowbridge develop a right-to-left and left-to-right barrel swing pattern that is so automatic that they are unable to hit an object thrown straight up into the air.

Of course, Tom knew the Major's reputation for safe-side wagering, but he was somewhat cagey himself and, besides, he figured it was worth a hundred dollars to find out what the Major had up his sleeve. He took the bet.

The following morning, Major Peabody uncased a 20-gauge shotgun. Before handing it to Tom Trowbridge, he removed the shell loaded with No. 7 chilled shot from the gun's chamber and replaced it with one containing a single slug. Then he walked ten yards to a boulder that was large enough for him to safely crouch behind. He threw his hat straight up into the air and waited for the shot that would double his cash reserve.

The story has a sad ending. The Major's favorite Irish tweed walking hat looked as if a giant moth had been at it. And he was one hundred dollars lighter. Trowbridge had let the Major's hat reach its zenith—and fall back to earth. Then he had very carefully aimed and ground-swatted it with the slug.

5

THE MAJOR'S (AND MONTEZUMA'S) REVENGE

WHEN TOM TROWBRIDGE DROVE Major Nathaniel Peabody to Phoenix he was in a jovial mood. Tom had wagered with him and won a hundred dollars—a rare occasion, indeed. And he had destroyed the Major's hat, which was a sort of satisfying repayment for some of the indignities that Peabody had visited upon him during previous hunts. The Major, in contrast, was in a definitely black and somber frame of mind. What he had engineered as a "sure-thing" bet had backfired, leaving him with less than ten dollars in his pocket.

Moreover, the Major's airline ticket to Hermosillo had been "borrowed" by a member of the Desert Bears hunt club—the banker who had learned his operations were being audited by the state. That banker, apparently, found it convenient to visit Mexico without notice and without leaving a clear track for the inquisitive to follow.

In a few days, the Major had to meet some of his Mexican friends at the Sonoran ranch of Dr. Mario Hernandez M. for a band-tailed pigeon hunt. To get from Phoenix to Hermosillo with less than ten dollars would be considered an unmanageable task by most of us. But the Major is at his imaginative best in this sort of challenging situation.

Once in Phoenix, Peabody donned his most worn suntans and spent a dollar at the St. Vincent de Paul Society store. He bought a suitcase that had seen better days. He packed some respectable clothing in it and went to the bus station, where he deposited his shotgun and the rest of his gear in a public locker. Then he made a phone call.

The Major's experience as a military attaché to various embassies in Latin America and his own half-Peruvian pedigree made it easy for him to effect the proper accent when he spoke to the Immigration and Naturalization Service. He informed the agent that there was an illegal alien hanging around the bus station.

Within an hour, Peabody was arrested. Two days later, after he turned down the offer of a grant of federal funds to attend the college of his choice, he was put on a bus and sent back to the place from whence (he told them) he had come—Hermosillo, in the State of Sonora, in the Republic of Mexico.

The Major later referred to this caper as "The Dry Back or Wet Front Maneuver."

At the Hermosillo bus station, after changing into more respectable clothing, he abandoned the disreputable suntans and beat-up suitcase. Peabody spent most of his remaining funds for a taxi ride to the airport and a telephone call to don Mario, who, shortly thereafter, appeared and welcomed his gringo friend to Mexico.

After the *abrazos* (manly hugs of greeting to the uninitiated)

Peabody explained his lack of luggage. Everyone knows it is the airlines' standard operating procedure to automatically misdirect hunters' weapons and baggage to such godless places as Sri Lanka, Outer Mongolia, or Detroit.

A thoughtful and cosmopolitan host, don Mario was more than pleased to supply the Major with a fine Spanish Arrieta sidelock double, a complete outfit of English shooting wear, and some "walking-around" money.

Don Mario appreciated the fact that Major Peabody had a gringo stomach. When the lining of such a stomach comes into contact with the Hermosillo water supply, it commonly produces great, terrible rumblings and another well-known and debilitating result that will keep the prudent man from straying more than a few meters from the lavatory—let alone journeying into the field for a pigeon hunt.

The electrolytically produced, pure H_2O that was available in don Mario's hacienda was perfectly safe. It was the same safe water that was provided in all the local hotels. But he knew the Major would not care to be limited to drinking only such safe liquid, so he provided a substantial supply of twelve-year old, unblended, malt, Scottish drinking fluid.

Early the next morning, three Land Rovers crowded with hunters drove through the arroyos and *ocotillo* to a place—between water and corn, manzanita berry and piñon—where herds of band-tailed pigeons were regularly observed.

The hunters were instructed to station themselves, partially concealed, at intervals not closer than one-and-a-half gun ranges apart. Since a disturbed band-tailed pigeon is apt to fly at head height, the determination of the length of "one-and-a-half gun

23

ranges" becomes more than merely an academic subject.

If the judgment of your neighbor is defective, you are well advised to bring the matter to his attention. An educational device occasionally employed by the Major consisted of firing in the direction of the erring neighbor. Many times the neighbor would quickly reconsider his distance estimate.

When the bandtail is on the wing, he tends to follow the lay of the land and loves to approach feeding areas by jetting through a pass or skyrocketing up one side of a ridge and down the other. His average cruising speed is estimated at forty-five miles an hour. When shot at, a flock of these birds reacts in a manner that can be confidently predicted. They will circle or plane or spiral or sail or rise or drop or continue on the same path, each (possibly) doing something different from the bird beside it, but all (probably) at twice their pre-shot-at speed.

For these reasons, the hunting of the band-tailed pigeon does not always produce joy and laughter. It has reduced many a quali-fied gunner to a mass of quivering jelly who, massaging an arm that is black and blue from shoulder to elbow from day-long firing, piteously sobs and begs his companions not to report his shooting display to anyone.

The Major shot well. It was his usual custom to adjust his mind to band-tailed pigeon shooting by presuming he was standing in a northern marsh, shooting at canvasback that were highballing downwind. Then he would increase the lead a bit. He had a great time and enjoyed the hunt. He also liked the companionship of Mario and the other hunters, as well as the food, the scotch, and— to be fair about it—the tequila, too. The hunt was extended for another week.

Much to my own relief, Peabody telephoned the Philadelphia offices of Smythe, Hauser, Engels & Tauchen. He authorized me to send his checks to Hermosillo. I had no desire to go to the Sonoran desert for personal delivery. The Major's army retirement and his trust remittance arrived before the extended hunt concluded, and the story had a happy ending.

In order not to inconvenience his host, Major Peabody spent the evening before his flight back to Phoenix at the Gran Hotel in Hermosillo. In the morning, as he entered the restaurant, he hear a hearty "halloo" and saw the banker who had absconded with his air ticket. He was smiling and waving the Major to his table to join him at breakfast.

The banker chuckled as he recounted how he had abstracted the Major's ticket in the dead of night. He truly enjoyed the joke. The Major smiled, but he did not laugh. The banker said he would be staying at the Gran Hotel for, perhaps, another week. By that time his attorneys would have negotiated reasonable settlements of any modest inconsistencies that might have been unearthed by the audit. He expected to soon be back in Arizona and looked forward to again hunting with the Major and the Desert Bears. He insisted on paying for the Major's breakfast, and the two parted in an amicable fashion.

When the Major returned to the lobby to arrange taxi transportation to the airport, he gave the manager US$50 in exchange for his solemn promise to serve the banker—at every meal—good old Hermosillo tap water, and, additionally, to make sure the water supply in the man's room was composed of the same stuff.

6

PROFESSOR PEABODY

I'M A CITY BOY, UNCOMFORTABLE WHENEVER buildings at least ten stories high are not in sight. Delivering checks to Peabody in the middle of a Guatemalan outback is not one of my favorite pastimes. On the other hand, such deliveries have taken me to various parts of the world and, I'll admit, have expanded my horizons and afforded me many interesting experiences that have aided in my education. Major Peabody has also been an important factor in educating me.

There is no guarantee that we get smarter merely because we get older. There is a difference between twenty years of experience and one year of experience twenty times. The quality of the experience and the presence of a good teacher are important if we are to learn to survive in a world filled with subterfuge, duplicity, and deception.

Major Peabody has been my professor. He once told me: "Someday, someone will give you ten-to-one odds that he can drop a coin on the cabin table and have it land and remain on it's narrow edge. Don't take the bet. You will lose. Only a sucker accepts a 'sure-fire' bet." It has taken me a long time to learn that lesson.

And I have paid for it. In education, as in other endeavors, there is no free lunch.

The costs of the Major's educational services have been high and include a substantial amount of money lost in betting and playing poker with him. I won't count the price of the boxes of imported cigars or the cases of single-malt Scotch whisky I've provided. In any event, on the twenty-eighth of a recent September a postcard (marked "Personal and Confidential") was received in the law offices of Smythe, Hauser, Engels & Tauchen, and delivered to me. The postcard informed me of the Major's proposed end-of-the-month whereabouts and demanded I be there for delivery of his October remittance.

And so, on the morning of the thirtieth of September, I arrived at the Austin Straubel Airport in Green Bay, Wisconsin. The Major had given his usual clear and accurate instructions for finding him (i.e., "Get to Highway 55. Then go north until you reach Alvin. Be careful. Don't miss it. It looks like a gas station and a grocery store. Ask them for directions to Tom Rosenow's cabin.").

From previous experience with the Major, I suspected the Rosenow cabin would be found somewhere on the back side of the moon and at the end of an unpaved, two-rutted logging road that looked like a poorly maintained otter slide. I considered renting a pulp skidder but settled for a four-wheel-drive pickup truck.

The directions for passage between Alvin and the grouse camp were as complicated as the steps of an eighteenth-century minuet. After three missed turns, I got to a log cabin. It was a beautiful structure located next to a sprawling reed- and tamarack-edged lake. There was electricity and a phone line.

It was the wrong cabin. The owner recognized my confusion.

He got into his pickup and led me to the final destination. When I arrived at the Rosenow cabin shortly before sundown, the Major and his hunting friends extended a cordial reception. Good food was followed by libation and conversation.

When my inexperience with shotguns and ruffed grouse was discovered, it was unanimously agreed these lapses in my education should be corrected. The next morning we convened behind the cabin. Tom Rosenow tacked a sheet of newspaper to a piece of thin plywood nailed to a nearby tree.

He gave me a .410 shotgun, and we backed off about twenty yards. He told me to hit the center of the newspaper. I followed instructions. The purpose of this exercise was to show the pattern produced by the gun. After a couple more tries—at fifteen and then ten yards—I hit the target and got a good idea of the area covered by the pellets.

Then the Major took over. He explained that the end of the barrel of the gun was the place where the shot came out. He warned me to never, never point it at any one and advised me that some of the local Forest County inhabitants were inclined to believe it might be better to let a bird escape than to wound a hunting companion.

He informed me the .410 was a particularly powerful weapon capable of shooting straight through a cement building block. I took the bait. Without thinking, I told them all that I doubted the little shotgun could shoot through a cement block. I had noticed that the pellets hadn't gone through the half-inch plywood target backing.

A cement block was produced and set atop a popple stump. A large black dot was marked in the center of its side. Major Peabody calmly stated that he could shoot through the block with the .410 using a shell loaded with No. 7½ chilled shot. He borrowed twenty dollars from Tom and laid it on the porch railing to emphasize the seriousness of his undertaking.

I should have known better than to accept the challenge. If I had thought for just a moment, I would have known I was about to become victimized by the operation of some quasi-fraud. But I was overcome by greed. It was part of my education, and it only cost me twenty dollars.

(Editor's note: Major Nathaniel Peabody has confirmed the essential accuracy of this report. He objects, however, to the term "quasi-fraud." He claims that the conditions of the wager were not violated in any way when he went to the popple stump and gave the cement block a quarter turn so he could see through the holes in its side. Then he put the barrel of the .410 through one of the holes and fired the weapon.)

7

UNCLE CALHOUN

"CALHOUN PEABODY WAS MY FAVORITE UNCLE," Major Nathaniel Peabody declared one evening as he helped himself to some more of his favorite single-malt Scotch whisky. I prefer white wines, myself, but since he once severely berated me for not doing so, I now keep a supply of The Glenlivet in my liquor cabinet.

I don't smoke. The Major is well aware of it. He gave me a humidor for Christmas. It was full of H. Upmann cigars. He suggested I keep it filled. Now, whenever he visits me, he knows he will be able to enjoy a fine imported cigar. And that is precisely what he did on this occasion. He removed one from the humidor, tested it with a gentle squeeze, nodded in approval, and returned to the overstuffed chair next to the fireplace in my Philadelphia apartment.

"He was, I suppose, some kind of a family black sheep," the Major continued as he lit the cigar and swirled the ice cubes in his glass. "You may find it difficult to believe," he mused, "but the Peabody family has produced a few black sheep." No one who knew the Major for even a short time would have any difficulty in believing that his family closet harbored black sheep.

"You see," he continued, "ever since the Peabodys went out of the plantation business over a hundred years ago, the men in the family were expected to become investment bankers or get into the diplomatic corps. The Peabodys have a long history of service to the government in international political affairs—and to themselves in matters financial.

"When Calhoun Peabody came of age and gave consideration to embarking upon a lifetime career, it didn't take him long to conclude that investment banking—and, for that matter, investment bankers—were dull and uninteresting. And he became convinced that the diplomatic corps was composed largely of men who squatted to pee.

"To the surprise of most of the family, and to the dismay and consternation of Great Aunt Aurora, Calhoun Peabody did not follow the family's historic occupational pattern. Instead, he became (as Great Aunt Aurora would sometimes be forced to admit) a person who sold things, a common tradesperson.

"Uncle Calhoun was not the first Peabody to break with family tradition. One of Great Aunt Aurora's cousins had his picture turned to the wall. She and the rest of the family were most reluctant to speak about him.

"It was Uncle Calhoun who finally identified the cousin and told me of his disgraceful and unforgivable act. He had become a United States senator. I still can't bring myself to pronounce the man's name in public. I am loath to believe anyone in my family could sink that low. I retain the hope that some terrible mistake has been made and the man has been wrongfully accused.

"In any event, black sheep or not, I liked Uncle Calhoun. During the 1930s, I was an inmate at military schools. I say 'schools' because two of them had absolutely no sense of humor and—ah—

asked me to retire. During these times, Uncle Calhoun came to my defense. And it was he who took me under his wing during school-vacation periods.

"Uncle Calhoun lived in Georgia. He taught me to use a shotgun. He taught me to hunt quail and appreciate hunting dogs. He gave direction to my life.

"He had a 1925-vintage, English-stocked, 20-gauge Lefever shotgun with twenty-four-inch barrels. It was his preferred quail gun and his pride and joy. But he let me use it. I would no more consider letting a teenager use my favorite shotgun than I would consider kissing one of those women who sing the Brunhilde roles in Wagnerian operas.

"Well, as I say, Uncle Calhoun loved to hunt quail. He spent most of his waking hours engaged in that sport or thinking about engaging in that sport. And at night, he dreamed about it.

"Though he amassed a substantial estate, he never gave me any advice or guidance in financial matters." Given Major Peabody's inability to manage money and his apparent disdain for investment, this admission came as no surprise to me. The Major went on with his description of his black-sheep uncle. "He considered the subjects essential to the proper education of a young man to be shotguns, dogs, and quail hunting. 'First things first,' he used to tell me. 'You can always hire some bean counter to manage your money.' "

I winced at that comment. The Major seemed not to notice and returned to his story.

"During the 1930s, things were not too rosy for the farm community. Neither were they very rosy for the insurance companies who had extended mortgage loans to the farm community. As a result, there were a lot of foreclosures, and the insurance companies ended up owning a lot of farms in Florida, Georgia, and South Carolina.

"Insurance company people tend to be stuffy types. They have an unfortunate penchant for erecting 'No Trespassing' signs and for prosecuting those who walk on their real-estate holdings. The admirable Christian philosophy of forgiving those who trespass against us is not an attitude they are willing to adopt.

"Now, Uncle Calhoun was deeply committed to the 'zero population growth' movement—at least insofar as it could be applied to quail populations. He sacrificed a lot of time and shells in supporting his position. He decided to teach me the intricacies of quail hunting because he thought the birds were getting ahead of him. He needed a trusty companion to help him keep their numbers under control. Of course, I accepted his offer.

"My uncle knew the locations of the abandoned farms. He knew those properties had not been disturbed by either farm machinery or hunters because the insurance companies owned them and enforced their 'No Trespassing' admonitions. *Quod erat demonstratum*, he reasoned quite accurately, coveys of quail could be found on them.

"Being well acquainted with the theorems of Thomas Robert Malthus, Uncle Calhoun knew the bird populations of those farms were increasing mightily. But if we were to hunt them without fear of reprisal from the district attorney's office, it would be necessary to reach an accommodation with the insurance companies vis-à-vis their injunction against walking on their property.

"In addition to the science of hunting, Uncle Calhoun taught me another valuable lesson: A little duplicity can go a long way. A local printer produced calling cards for him. Then he visited the home offices of the insurance companies that had been most active in the foreclosure of area farms. He presented himself as a licensed real-estate agent and solicited the listings of the foreclosed properties.

"The insurance companies were overjoyed to find someone who might help them unload nonproductive assets of such questionable value as represented by the unused farmland. Uncle Calhoun got broad authority to enter, evaluate, and show their properties to potential purchasers.

"Whenever Calhoun Peabody entered the aforesaid abandoned farms, he was accompanied by a bird dog, and he always carried his Lefever 20-gauge shotgun for protection against the potential of assault by person or persons unknown. I was the prospective buyer who was most often shown the lands.

"Uncle Calhoun's circle of acquaintances was composed almost entirely of quail hunters. They, too, became 'prospective buyers.' They'd spend days walking abandoned farms with their 'agent,' investigating and evaluating the properties. They, too, walked behind dogs and carried shotguns.

"After spending a weekend with Uncle Calhoun, one of his cronies, a dentist from Nashville, actually inquired about buying a farm for a quail-hunting retreat. Calhoun Peabody promptly got a real estate agent's license, sold the farm, and earned a commission.

"By thus engaging in a 'trade,' he became a family black sheep and a disappointment to Great Aunt Aurora. But, over the years, he spent a lot of time hunting and, incidentally, became one of the most successful real-estate agents in the Southeast.

"Every one of his clients was a quail hunter."

8

THE ORDER OF THE TARANTULA

AFTER HE RECEIVED HIS COMMISSION AS a second lieutenant in the United States Army, Nathaniel Peabody was sent to Central America. It was during the Second World War, and Lieutenant Peabody was assigned to serve as the military attaché at our embassy in the Republic of Anchuria.

The assignment was entirely appropriate. Peabody was born in Bogota, in the Republic of Colombia. He was half Peruvian. He was fluent in the Spanish language. Peabody understood and appreciated the customs and culture of Latin Americans. In contrast to our then ambassador to Anchuria, he had the temperament and ability to quickly develop a wide circle of Anchurian friends.

The ambassador was from Ohio and, before assuming the embassy post, had never left the Midwest. He was a prosperous widget manufacturer. During the 1940 presidential elections, he contributed mightily to the Committee to Reelect Franklin D. Roosevelt.

When that momentous event occurred, the manufacturer

demanded a government position as an appropriate recognition of his financial support. After much hesitation and soul searching, he was given a job, but only on the condition that he leave the United States and live in a country where he had little opportunity to embarrass the Roosevelt administration.

With congressional approval and acquisition of the august title of ambassador to the Republic of Anchuria, the man became even more pompous. But he was smart enough to recognize his own lack of experience. To compensate for that shortcoming, he came to rely on the advice and direction of the British ambassador.

The American ambassador was a teetotaler. Prior to the unionization, of the Universal Widget Company, an employee discovered drinking on or off the job was peremptorily fired. The ambassador did not hunt. He considered hunting to be barbaric and those who committed the act to be uncivilized. The ambassador did not play poker. To him, gambling—in any form—was anathema.

Before Lieutenant Peabody left for Anchuria, a friend in the U.S. State Department warned him of the ambassador's peculiarities. Peabody knew his first tour of duty would be difficult, bordering on the impossible. During the early years of the Second World War, U-boats were sinking ships in the Caribbean Sea. They were freighters bound for the States, carrying oil from Venezuela and bauxite from Jamaica. When Lieutenant Peabody wondered aloud about the possibility of German U-boats refueling in some little-known Anchurian bay and suggested an appropriate investigation, the ambassador ordered him to map the coastline and find every place where the brutal Hun or the hated Jap could supply a submarine or land an invasion force.

The ambassador was insensitive to the fact that he was in a sovereign foreign land and needed appropriate authorization from his host country. Peabody suggested it might be prudent to secure the approval of the Anchurian military and involve them in the project. The ambassador reluctantly agreed.

Lieutenant Peabody got the cooperation of a captain in the Anchurian army. The two of them and a young man from the capital hired indigenous Indians to pole them up and down the coastal regions in dugout canoes.

Two-week expeditions were not uncommon, and the lieutenant and his companions regularly revisited areas that had especially dangerous potential. Peabody's reports were detailed, extensive, and accompanied by sketches and geographical notations. Washington took notice.

The ambassador was uncomfortable when he read the effusive praise for the lieutenant's coastal-mapping initiatives. He was jealous of Peabody's popularity with the locals. And he was decidedly nervous when his young wife and the lieutenant got together at various embassy social functions. He decided he had better find a reason to get rid of his military attaché. A quiet investigation of Peabody's activities began.

The ambassador found that one of Lieutenant Peabody's Washington requisitions asked for three Purdey shotguns. This didn't seem noteworthy. The ambassador thought maybe shotguns were the better weapons for the kind of fighting Peabody might encounter in his survey sorties into the coastal jungles.

Then he discovered the number of cases of 12-gauge No. 4 and No. 6 shotgun shells that were periodically included in the embassy's incoming diplomatic pouches. None of the lieutenant's reports mentioned any situations involving unfriendly fire. And the British ambassador revealed that there were only twelve Nazis in the entire country. They operated the local brewery and were all harmless, old, World War I veterans. The American ambassador became suspicious.

He asked an Anchurian, employed as a cook for the embassy dining hall, to secretly follow Peabody and report his activities. The cook liked Peabody. He didn't want to get the young man in any kind of trouble, but he had a job to do. He tried to put the right spin on his report, as follows: "Lieutenant Peabody and two others left the capital in the embassy Jeep at noon on Tuesday. The Jeep also contained four cases of shotgun shells, one case of scotch, and three shotguns.

"The three men arrived at Cayo Gordo in the evening and, early the next morning, they hired three Indios with dugout canoes to pole them through the mangroves to the part of the bay they wanted to map. In order to hide from any inquisitive Nazi who might have been in the vicinity, the Indios macheted off tree shoots and underbrush and built hiding places for the three mappers. Then the Indios left in their canoes.

"I believe the Indios became separated and lost. Every half hour or so I could hear them signaling each other by pounding on the sides of the canoes with their paddles and shouting.

"Consistently, the air would soon be filled with flocks of teal, bluebill, and an occasional pintail, all of which would attack the three mapmakers. The three of them would jump up from their hiding places, fire their shotguns, and shoo the ducks away. But soon the pounding would begin again, the ducks would return, and the three men would have to chase them away again. I don't know how they were able to get any work done at all.

"In the late afternoon, all six returned to the village. There are many snakes in the area, and they may have been bitten. They were all taking medicine—some with water, others straight.

"This pattern was repeated for days, but the lieutenant did not tire, nor did his efforts flag. He and his friends kept right on mapping, day after day, stopping only after they had run out of shells or snakebite medicine. I couldn't see which. Then they returned to the capital."

The ambassador read the report a few times and suspected that Peabody was hunting ducks. He took his theory to his British counterpart who confirmed it. The American ambassador was elated. In one fell swoop he would destroy Peabody's reputation in Washington and at the same time, perhaps, have him sent to the Russian front.

The ambassador enjoyed preparing his exposé of Lieutenant Peabody. He was on his third rewrite when the secretary to the president of the republic invited him to the palace. The president told the ambassador of the great respect he and his chief of staff had for Lieutenant Peabody and his coastal mapping. Then the president announced that the lieutenant would receive the highest honor his country could bestow on a foreigner—the Order of the Tarantula.

The perplexed ambassador explained his problem to his British friend. It was the British ambassador who told him that he could not expose Peabody. After the republic had bestowed its highest honor on the attaché, any disgrace that befell the lieutenant would be considered a humiliating slap in the president's face and would publicly cast doubt on the competence of the republic's chief of staff. It would destroy relations between Anchuria and the United States.

The British ambassador told his American counterpart that Peabody couldn't be disgraced, but perhaps the receipt of the great honor could be used to have the lieutenant assigned to another country—perhaps someplace in South America would be far enough.

And that's how Peabody received the Order of the Tarantula. And that's how he became a first lieutenant. And that's how he was transferred to the embassy in Bogota, Colombia.

The United States ambassador was never told that only one Order of the Tarantula was ever bestowed. He never learned that the duck-hunting Anchurian army captain was the president's favorite nephew. He didn't know that the other duck hunter in the party was the son of the British ambassador or that the British ambassador, himself, was an avid duck hunter. He didn't appreciate how strong were the bonds that join duck hunters. He didn't know Peabody had lost interest in his young wife. He had no idea how he had been maneuvered into a position where he not only had to commend the lieutenant's work and suggest promotion, but also get him sent to Colombia, the country with the best dove shooting in the world.

9

The Major and the Truth

"I'VE ALWAYS CONTENDED THAT REASONABLE honesty is the best policy" said Major Nathaniel Peabody as he sat in my apartment and sipped some of The Glenlivet that I thought (erroneously) I had successfully hidden under the sink in my kitchen. The Major was unaware of the expression of extreme disbelief that came over me. That expression did not change as he continued his monologue.

"Though many of my friends have often encouraged me to tell untruths, I have consistently resisted all such suggestions. Arthur Van Brunt was one who tried to lead me into a pattern of perjury. Arthur was a wonderful old gentleman and an excellent pass shooter. He had access to some of the best waterfowl-hunting territory in Maryland.

"I enjoyed his company, and we were the best of friends. We spent many hours together in duck and goose blinds. Arthur became my father-in-law, and I liked him so much I never rebuked him for introducing me to his daughter. Frankly, I'll never understand how a woman whose father was such a fine wingshot could harbor such strange prejudices against cigars and be more interested in cocktail parties and the opera than in dogs and shotguns.

43

"The evening before I married Elizabeth—or perhaps I should say the evening before Elizabeth married me—her father suggested I feign an epileptic seizure. It would, he said, give me time to seriously reconsider the proposed nuptials. He feared that matrimony might restrict our joint duck-hunting expeditions.

"Time proved the wisdom of his advice. I should have listened to him, but I did not. I simply could not bring myself to change my long-established policy of refusing to engage in subterfuge." That last statement took me so completely by surprise that I choked and spit out some of my highball.

"So, at the appointed hour and place, I told the then truth and said, 'I do.' The marriage lasted little more than a year." The Major paid no attention to my reaction to his denial of engaging in subterfuge.

"Elizabeth and I were highly incompatible. You see, she was a woman, and I was a man. When there are differences of such an obvious magnitude, marriages seldom work out.

"On the credit side of the ledger, it must be said Arthur also introduced me to Mollie. Mollie was loyal. She accepted me as I was. She was faithful. She never argued or peddled guilt. And she loved to hunt. She was the best Chesapeake Bay retriever I ever owned.

"I'm told by those who are supposed to know about such things that friendships seldom develop between two females if either or both consider the other to be a threat. In spite of Arthur's and my attempts to bring them together, Elizabeth and Mollie never seemed to hit it off.

"And the fault was evenly divided. Elizabeth entered strenuous objections to the presence of Mollie's hair on her furniture. She even suggested Mollie refrain from sleeping on our bed.

"Mollie, on the other hand, showed her dissatisfaction by once irrigating Elizabeth's leg in the middle of the living room during a well-attended afternoon social affair.

"Mollie and Arthur and I were able to continue our out-of-doors pursuits, but with diminishing frequency—a situation that brought discomfort to all three of us. Arthur would propose wild and imaginative scenarios designed to mask our hunting trips. However, I maintained my standards and never used a falsehood in arranging to participate in them.

"I recall explaining a planned ten-day absence that was to be occasioned by a Canadian duck hunt. Arthur had suggested I mask the trip by saying I thought I had cancer and was going to the Mayo Clinic for a checkup. Naturally, I eschewed the advice. I told Elizabeth that my dear Aunt Carlota in Lima was in very bad shape and that it would be improper for me to stay in Bryn Mawr during such a trying time. It was a truthful statement. Aunt Carlota was, indeed, in very bad shape. She had been dead for seven years.

"As I've said, Mollie and Elizabeth didn't get along. There was almost constant conflict between them. It culminated during the final months of our union. Elizabeth had a heavy golden bracelet that she treasured. It was her customary but not invariable practice to remove it and place it on the nightstand. Next, she would repeat her complaint about Mollie's presence and insist the dog be kicked off the bed. Then she would go to sleep.

"Elizabeth awoke one morning and couldn't find the bracelet. She was quite disturbed about the loss. It became a matter of great concern and endless commentary on her part. My assurances that I had not pawned the bracelet in order to finance the purchase of a Charles Daly side-by-side 10-gauge goose gun were of no avail.

"I spent two full days searching for the damned thing and finally found it—thereby bringing relative peace and tranquillity to the household. When Elizabeth questioned where I found it, I temporized and changed the subject.

"Arthur warned me that his daughter's female curiosity would not rest until she learned where the bracelet had been discovered. He advised me to say it had been entwined in the bedsprings. This was not the truth, and I would not tell a lie. But, again, Arthur was right. The pressure for disclosure was tremendous.

"As the sun rose on the next Saturday morning, the duck-hunting season opened. I missed it because I was obliged to attend an afternoon concert by the Philadelphia Philharmonic Orchestra. During the concert intermission, I was herded into the lobby. There Elizabeth showed her friends the antique bracelet, recounting her anguish at its disappearance and her joy upon its unexplained recovery. In front of them all, she demanded I tell how I found it.

"Now, I'll admit I was a bit piqued. Arthur and Mollie were hunting, and I was not. If I had not been disgruntled I might have found a way to sidestep Elizabeth's question. But I made no attempt to do so. I told the truth.

" 'Apparently Mollie was aware of Elizabeth's attachment to the bracelet,' " I explained. 'Angry at being shoved off the bed and in a fit of jealousy, the dog had eaten it. While cleaning Mollie's kennel, I found the bracelet embedded in a pile of dog residue.'

"With a certain amount of pride I reported how I hosed it off and presented it to my soul mate. And, I added, if they looked carefully between the links, they might still find positive evidence of the truth of my statement.

"Elizabeth became unaccountably upset and filed for divorce the next day.

"Since then, Arthur has gone to his reward. I miss him. Still, had I followed his advice and lied, I might still be married to Elizabeth. That marriage caused me many an anxious, disagreeable, and stressful moment. If it had not been for my insistence on the truth, my ship of life might still be sailing in turbulent waters.

"Yes, my boy, honesty is the best policy."

10

DUCK HUNTING IN HONDURAS

MAJOR PEABODY HELD THE REMAINS of his other-than-first glass of unblended scotch and water in one hand and used the other to rescue a dead branch from the supply of dry wood collected by his fellow hunters for the night's campfire. He poked it into the embers. After a bit, he retrieved it and lit his cigar with the coal that now glowed from the end of the stick.

It had been a good day in the field. It was late October. The leaves were beginning to show their fall colors. The hunters had found grouse. As the crisper evening temperatures overtook the Indian summer afternoon, the talk turned from grouse to ducks. And the Major was in an expansive mood.

"Lesser scaup and ringbill winter in the northern part of Central America," he said, rattling the ice cubes as a signal for one of the younger men to provide a replacement. "Occasionally a pintail will show itself, and there is a strange local duck known as a *pinchinida* and sometimes called a *pinchi*.

"The *pinchi.* flies at an estimated speed of two-and-a-half miles per hour, and its legs tend to hang down. It is vaguely reminiscent of a World War II B29 bomber with its landing gear exposed. It hits the water with one helluva splash.

"There are a lot of ducks flying around on the Caribbean coasts of Belize and Honduras. If that fact isn't enough to whet your appetite, and if you need further motivation, there are other good reasons for a Central American duck hunt.

"First of all, down there the season opens about the time ours closes. And the hunting extends into March, the time of year when our scatterguns are normally unused and forgotten, clearly in violation of an injunction that, I believe, is contained somewhere in Holy Scripture, or, at least, in the Boy Scout oath.

"Second, it simply isn't morally correct to allow our weapons to stand lonely, unloved, and decaying in a gun cabinet during the winter months. They should be carried to Honduras where they can enjoy the climate and engage in honest employment.

"And finally, after being chilled to nearly absolute zero while cringing in a blind on some northern lake, you can fly to Central America and hunt in shirt sleeves in tropical temperatures. This will renew your faith that the world is organized in a rational manner—despite the overwhelming evidence to the contrary."

The Major was quietly promoting a trip to hunt ducks in Honduras. He was certain some of his friends would want to join him. So he waited to hear the statements he knew would be made. In seconds, they came. "Sounds great Major. If you're going, I'll go with you."

Another voice said, "Me, too." And a third added, "Count me in. And I'm sure Doc Carmichael will want to come."

Major Peabody moved his canvas chair back from the campfire just a bit. The smoke quickly changed direction and, instead of coming toward him, wafted into the eyes of his companions. "I sus-pect Doc Carmichael won't want to join us," said Peabody. "He's been there before, you know. He took the trip more than twenty years ago."

The hunters expected a story from the Major. They weren't dis-appointed.

"The Doc and I planned to go to Honduras for a midwinter duck hunt rather than stay in Philadelphia and enjoy its delightful February weather. Due to an unforeseen last-moment develop-ment—a particularly disastrous evening at the poker table—I was unable to accompany him.

"The Doc had rescheduled his surgeries and office appoint-ments, purchased his air transportation, and arranged to write off the costs as a business expense on his income-tax return. He decided to go by himself. I had a friend in La Ceiba, the doctor's port of entry. I called him and told him of the arrival. Hernando said he'd meet Doc at the airport customs house and deliver him to the hunt guide.

Carmichael figured a trip to Central America was a lot like going to Hudson's Bay. You brought your weapons, some single-malt Scotch whisky, and a handful of money for licenses, lodging, food, guiding expenses, et cetera. Since Doc didn't speak Spanish, he didn't think he'd be spending much on the et cetera.

"Doc didn't have an extensive knowledge of the history, cul-ture, or social attitudes of the folks who live in Central America. Putting it another way, he didn't really understand that anyone who brought a firearm into Honduras in 1978 was sure to be sus-pected of planning to assassinate *el presidente*. And, nine times out of ten, the suspicion was well founded.

"Of course, Doc's intention was to pass-shoot the large population of local and wintering scaup. Assassinating *el presidente* was fairly low on his list of priorities. But there was a serious communication problem, and it caused difficulties.

"The doctor knew three words in Spanish: *cerveza, senorita,* and *si.* But he was convinced he could make himself understood if he used English, enunciated clearly, and spoke loudly. This theory went to hell in a hurry. He got into trouble before he could get through customs.

"He figured something had gone wrong when they put handcuffs on him and marched him off to the local bastille for interrogation. My Honduran friend was waiting at the airport, but when he saw the Doc in handcuffs and the guardia leading him toward the jailhouse, he concluded that it would be prudent to avoid involvement, so he calmly walked off in another direction.

"At the jail, the *comandante*'s ability to speak English was almost as good as the Doc's command of Spanish. He knew the words "hello," "my dear," and "yes." However, during the questioning, the *comandante* smiled a lot and as long as he kept smiling, Doc Carmichael, believing *cerveza* and *senorita* were not relevant to the conversation, kept saying, *si,* and smiling back.

"This turned out to be a mistake. It didn't take long before Doc's '*si*' answer to one of the questions resulted in an explosively indignant look on the *comandante*'s face and, in a very few minutes, the doctor found himself against an adobe wall. His hands were tied behind his back. A bunch of soldiers were lined up with their rifles pointing at him, and the *comandante*, with an upraised sword, was standing at their side, yelling, '*listo . . . apunte . . .*'

"Meanwhile, my Honduran friend had learned that his

mother-in-law was coming for a weekend visit. It was a convenient time for him to go duck hunting, so he had driven to the *comandancia* to try to straighten things out for the doctor. His timing was excellent.

"The firing squad had missed twice, and the sergeant had just returned from the general store with another box of rifle cartridges. After a full, well-translated explanation and the Doc's assignment of his two bottles of single-malt scotch to the *comandante*, he was released from custody.

"I never learned any of the details of his hunt. Whenever I mention Honduras, the Doc seems to stiffen up. He doesn't talk much about it, but I get the impression he doesn't want to go back. Maybe the ducks weren't flying."

Dear Major Peabody

MAJOR NATHANIEL PEABODY WAS IN a dark mood. His afternoon mail brought a letter from the Audubon Society. He had waited for that letter with more than modest anticipation. When he recognized the society's logo on one of the letters, he immediately tore it open, dropping the envelope and the rest of the mail on the floor.

As he hurriedly read the correspondence, his face fell and he was, indeed, disappointed. His expectations, clearly, were unfulfilled. The letter said:

Dear Major Peabody,

Your recent letter was forwarded to me for evaluation and response. I have been active in the Audubon Society for over thirty years and have studied and written extensively on the *Bonasa umbellus* family. I am considered to be an authority on the ruffed grouse.

Your stated interest in the preservation of this species is duly noted and, under normal circumstances, would probably be applauded. Your stated interest in the creation of forest habitat specifically suitable for the development of a more extensive ruffed-grouse population, on the surface at least, appears to be admirable, as is your offer for the use of privately owned forest lands for the experiment.

I emphasize the phrase "on the surface." I am authorized to tell you the proposal that this organization undertake the expenditure of substantial sums of money to produce improved ruffed-grouse habitat in the particular areas you identify is not a suggestion this organization can support. And, I personally assure you that we will not even consider it as long as I am alive.

Of course, you are well aware of the reason for this immediate and permanent—I repeat, *permanent*—refusal of your proposal. But, just for the record, let me be more specific.

First of all, no one with more than a kindergartner's knowledge of the ruffed grouse could, without surprise, read your reference to "the increasingly rare but beautiful sound of the ruffed grouse at sunrise, with its clearly melodious and trilling song." Suffice it to say that this entirely inaccurate and silly statement attracted my attention.

Call me skeptical, if you wish, but my curiosity caused me to make inquiries. The investigation showed you are not the owner of the tracts of land in Maine, Wisconsin, Upper Michigan, and Minnesota where you want us to establish the habitat experiment. My inquiries further showed these lands are owned by others who use them as private grouse-hunting camps.

The investigation also revealed you to be a well-known bird hunter and one who is frequently invited to aforesaid camps, where you, yourself, engage in that unspeakable shotgunning activity that depletes the ruffed-grouse population.

It is the considered opinion of the society that the proposal included within your letter is nothing more than a poorly conceived façade masking an attempt to use our organization's funds to support your own personal hunting proclivities—nothing more and nothing less.

It is a pleasure to deny your request.

Sincerely, etc.

The Major was irritated by the tone of the letter. "Poorly designed, indeed," he snorted as he crumpled it and threw it into the fireplace.

A few days later, the mails brought a response to another of the letters earlier sent out by the Major. It came from the Friends and Protectors of Inhuman Species (FPIS). The letter did nothing to alleviate Peabody's continued depression. Like the one from the Audubon Society, the contents of the FPIS letter were not satisfactory. It said:

Dear Major Peabody,

Thank you for your letter and your concern for the endangered ruffed grouse. To think that, all too soon, no one may again hear the sweet song of the Grouse at sunrise is a most frightening prospect. Your offer to provide forest land in various states certainly shows you are a caring person, truly dedicated to the preservation of the environment and the protection of our feathered friends.

We here at the Friends and Protectors of Inhuman Species have not yet been able to actually develop land or spend any money to create appropriate animal habitat. We are, thus, unable to take advantage of your generous offer.

But we salute you. Your name has been added to the list of those who will be considered to receive our coveted and prestigious annual Great Auk Award.

As you may be aware, the needs of we who protect all nonhuman things are many. There is so much to be done. And our expenses are so great. The FPIS enjoys a well-deserved reputation for educating the masses about the threats and dangers they face. Each year, in the thousands and thousands of letters we send in our constant fund-raising drives, we enclose a page describing the bugs, worms, weeds, and other things that may disappear from the Earth.

We barely have enough money to pay our own substantial salaries and buy the company autos we all get to use. When you add the amount of money we need to mail all those fund-raising letters and print that extra page, well, you can see we have a serious problem.

A donation form is attached to this letter. We look forward to receiving an annual contribution from you. Our corporation enjoys a tax-free designation from the Internal Revenue Service. The money you send to us is deductible on both your federal and state income tax return. . . .

Major Peabody read no farther. He was about to assign the letter to the wastebasket but decided against it. Instead, he reinserted it into its envelope, which he carefully resealed. Then he wrote, "Deceased—Return to Sender," on the face of the envelope and put it with his outgoing mail.

During the following week, black scenarios crowded the Major's thoughts—man's inhumanity to man, the incomprehensible lack of proper priorities in the so-called charitable organizations, the down cycles of the ruffed grouse. But then he received a letter from the Centers for Disease Control in Atlanta. It read:

Dear Major Peabody,

Thank you for your letter. We have reviewed its contents with interest. Please be assured we here at the Centers for Disease Control sincerely appreciate your most generous offer for the use of private lands for the experiments therein set forth.

The Centers for Disease Control are definitely sensitive to the victims of all sickness and, in particular, to those who have contracted Lyme Disease. The report you sent to us, showing that the ruffed grouse eats huge amounts of the wood ticks that carry the disease, may well be the key to ending the suffering caused by that malady.

We are very pleased to advise you that our director is enthusiastic about your Wood Tick Control Proposal. He has already created the required additional bureaucracy on paper and has transferred the funds needed to build office space, hire additional personnel, and put the proposal into operation.

Since neither liberal nor conservative congresspersons

have the courage to delete any budget item that suggests it might result in even an insignificant reduction in the incidence of Lyme Disease, we may all be assured that additional funding will be approved during next year's congressional budget hearings

We will actively pursue the methods you suggest for building the population of the tick-eating ruffed grouse and the resultant eradication of the dreaded Lyme Disease. Clover plantings and the elimination of ruffed-grouse predators will begin on the Wisconsin lands as soon as possible, with work in Upper Michigan, Maine, and Minnesota following at a later date.

The Major reread the letter and smiled. He recalled the old adage: "Patience and perseverance made a bishop of His Reverence."

---- 12 ----

A Modest Proposal

IT WAS EARLY IN OCTOBER. THE PUDDLE DUCKS—the local teal and mallards—hadn't yet decided to fly south. They'd stay until colder temperatures and blustery winds made them move on. Major Nathaniel Peabody knew he, too, should have waited for those conditions before hunting ducks, but it had been over ten months since he had sat in a blind. And he was too anxious.

The Major was in a well-constructed shore blind at the end of a long finger of land pointing toward the middle of a lake. His shotgun leaned against a shelf in front of him. On that shelf, a thermos bottle filled with tomato soup and an open box of shells containing No. 4 chilled steel shot were placed within easy reaching distance.

From that point of land, a duck hunter wearing chest waders could walk out and set his decoys without needing a boat. An eighth-of-a-mile walk back into the woods would bring him to the cabin, where the woodstove might still hold heat. It was a very comfortable setup. It was one of the better-planned and better-situated blinds on the lake.

The Labrador seemed to be asleep on the flooring of the blind, and the Major's hunting companion leaned back on the bench and dozed. The prospects for the hunt were not good. It was a bluebird day. Moreover, a pan fisherman had anchored his rowboat between the decoys and the center of the lake. Unfortunately, thought the Major, his location is about one-and-a-half times the range of my 12-gauge.

Any vagrant duck that might otherwise have been attracted by the decoys wouldn't come close to the set because of that fisherman and his boat. So, Major Peabody stopped concentrating on duck hunting. His mind moved to other matters. He nudged his fellow hunter into consciousness and engaged him in a one-sided conversation.

"The historians tell us," he said, "that the northern European Celts of the first century A.D. would save up their condemned criminals and throw a big party every five years. During the celebrations, as a sacrifice to the gods, they'd garrote those prisoners and throw them into peat bogs.

"The ceremony was supposed to protect the rest of the Celts from the power of sorcerers. As Christianity was introduced to the pagans, the more civilized practice of burning witches at the stake was used to accomplish the same end. No one has been sacrificed to the Celtic gods for well over a thousand years, and the last witches were burned by the so-called advanced cultures of the mid-1600s in our own state of Massachusetts. I bring these matters to your attention for a reason. They are instructive.

"Not a single instance of even one real witch being found in northern Europe or in Massachusetts has been reliably reported since those times. It must be concluded that the cooking of witches and the Celtic ritualistic garroting have been amazingly successful in protecting us all from witchcraft.

"Apparently a number of gods have been propitiated through the practice of human sacrifice. The Nahuacs of central Mexico hauled their elected victims to the tops of truncated pyramids and there butchered them with obsidian knives. There was nothing personal in it. They just wanted to make sure the sun would continue to revolve around the earth.

"One cannot help but conclude that the ritual has been effective. Thanks to it, the sun has continued to shine for the benefit of us all—even though there have been no such Aztec ceremonies since the days of Cortez.

"Though human sacrifice has fallen into disrepute in recent years, there's a lot to be said in its favor. Certainly the effective elimination of witchcraft and the maintaining of the planet in sunlight are no small accomplishments. And now that more and more states are invoking capital punishment as a method for alleviating the terribly overcrowded conditions in our prisons, it occurs to me that there is an excellent opportunity to improve the state of hunting, our favorite sport.

"Instead of merely killing off condemned criminals in some sterile prison chamber, our lawmakers should recognize the advantages of the ancient practice of ritual murder and substitute provisions for the sacrifice of those who have met the legislative standards for capital punishment. Our elected officials could dedicate the sacrifice of murderers to Diana, the goddess of the hunt. It very well might be one of the few, if not the only, praiseworthy laws passed during their terms of office.

Elected representatives could not only assure their constituents of successful hunting seasons but could also become popular with the many outdoorsmen who vote. This might even assure them of attaining their most avidly desired goal—reelection.

"Federal legislators could require spies to be burned at the stake and their ashes sent to Georgia. There, with proper cabalistic incantation, the remains would be scattered over farmlands while supplication is made to the appropriate gods to grant the successful production and hatching of large clutches of quail eggs.

"I don't believe any civilized person would oppose a human sacrifice to that happy god Bacchus if it resulted in the distillation and distribution of quality Scotch drinking whisky. And while we're at it, do you happen to know which goddess is in charge of good cigars?

"Just think of the potential uses for sacrificial victims at Ducks Unlimited raffles. Win one at a drawing and, at your favorite lake, he will be sacrificed to the goddess in charge of growing wild rice or of giving proper leads while pass-shooting ducks.

"It wouldn't take long before other organizations would want to participate. The chamber of commerce could slaughter and sacrifice someone for favorable treatment by the God of Commercial Expansion in the Face of Increasing Corporate Taxation. The library board could get special help in collecting fines and recovering overdue books.

"Of course, if the new capital-punishment/human-sacrifice laws provide only for the killing of spies and homicidal maniacs, there won't be enough victims to go around—thus flying in the face of supply-side economics. Disaster could result. We should all assume our responsibilities to the republic and help our lawmakers by recommending others who are proper subjects for extermination.

"The first bunch to come to mind are defeated politicians.

When in office, all of them undoubtedly committed serious high crimes and misdemeanors, and deserve extinction. Moreover, their demise will help balance the budget and remove a drain from the treasury. By polishing them off, we will automatically terminate the fat retirement payments they voted for themselves.

"And," said the Major, ignoring the fact that his hunting partner had returned to his dozing, "when you write to your lawmaker naming those who should be terminally punished, please make special mention of those [expletive deleted] fishermen who anchor their [expletive deleted] rowboats near duck hunters' decoys."

13

Dog Story

IT WAS IN IOWA. IT WAS IN THE LATE AFTERNOON. It was after a pheasant hunt. Major Nathaniel Peabody and three of his hunting friends were seated in front of the lodge's huge fireplace in an attitude of relaxation. The dog-owning hunters were bragging about their animals.

It was easy to see they were experienced hunters. Anyone who brags about his dog's abilities before the hunt is, obviously, an amateur. Invariably, that man's dog will misbehave. And that inexperienced hunter will become experienced. He will become the object of unmerciful ridicule when the cigars and the post-hunt libations have been distributed.

His pre-hunt bragging will have destroyed any chance he may have had to use the time-honored excuse, "She's only a puppy." Experienced hunters brag about their dogs *after* the hunt.

Major Peabody did not own a hunting dog. Dog ownership is difficult for a person who lives in a Philadelphia apartment and spends a lot of time in airplanes traveling to distant hunting arenas. Some years earlier, the Major had reluctantly parted company with his own Chesapeake after finding her a suitable home with a Delaware duck hunter.

The Best of the Major

Because he didn't have a dog, the Major was often selected as the referee whenever dog arguments erupted in camp. He would offer supporting commentary to a hunter whose dog was subjected to intense criticism and gently deflate one whose bragging became a bit extreme. Major Peabody loved all dogs and liked a level playing field.

In the afterglow of the last day of that Iowa pheasant hunt, a discussion of breed intelligence evolved. Arguments favoring the Labrador retriever, the English setter, and the Brittany were all advanced. Strangely enough, the dogs owned by the three hunters who filed briefs were a Labrador retriever, an English Setter, and a Brittany. Unable to reach agreement as to which was the most intelligent, the parties appealed to Major Peabody. They asked him to decide. Peabody understood the gravity of the situation. He had been placed in a very uncomfortable position. Each of the hunters was convinced, far beyond reasonable doubt, that his own dog was the best in the entire world.

To suggest to such a man that another dog is superior to his is like saying his daughter is ugly. Worse, in fact. Daughters seldom retrieve to hand. If the Major favored one of the dogs, he would endear himself to one of the hunters, thus ensuring his future invitations to hunt with that individual and, more importantly, with his hunting dog. But Peabody would also alienate two other hunters and ruin his potential future association with them and, more importantly, with *their* hunting dogs.

However, the ball was in his court. After studying the contents of his empty glass, rattling the ice cubes and noticing one of the hunters (the one with the English setter) rise and begin to construct a replacement for him, Major Nathaniel Peabody said,

"Breed intelligence has been debated for centuries.

"In developing dogs for specific purposes, be it herding sheep or digging out badgers, the intelligence of the particular animal has always been a prime consideration when selecting breeding pairs. This careful breeding is the reason hunting dogs have superior intellect. The question before the house this afternoon really is: Which of these three particular dogs is the smartest?

"In reaching a decision, one must be careful to consider the particular animal's ability to recognize and compensate for any of its own particular deficiencies," said the Major, watching the expressions of his companions.

He saw the hunters looking a bit disturbed at the implied suggestion that one of their dogs might have a deficiency. Then he quickly added, "If any." His friends didn't change their stern looks. Clearly, if the Major so much as mentioned the particular deficiencies of any one of these dogs, he would be in deep trouble. So, he offered the additional explanation: "Such ability, of course, would be a sign of intelligence."

Peabody again looked at his companions and again recognized their negative and defensive reactions to what they interpreted as an accusation that their dogs were not perfect. He now ran the risk of alienating all three of them. This was not what he had in mind.

He temporized by taking a sip of his scotch and water while he thought of a way to escape. What would Solomon do? He thought. "Let me give you an example," he said, ignoring the collective frowns.

"Back in the late 1930s, my uncle, Calhoun Peabody, lived in a rural part of southern Georgia. One day, a half-starved and obviously lost or abandoned dog appeared at his back door. It was a combination beagle, black-and-tan coonhound, and heaven knows what else. Uncle Calhoun took the animal in and fed it.

"The dog, being cared for, was smart enough to remain near the house. I stayed with Uncle Calhoun during the summer months when military school was not in session. I formed a close attachment to the animal. The dog had no hunting instincts whatsoever. It became a house pet. I called it 'Sporty.'

"Though Sporty received the attentions of a veterinarian, he began to lose his eyesight and was soon completely blind. Uncle Calhoun, in deference to me, I'm sure, did not put Sporty down. He knew I loved the dog.

"Well, gentlemen, this animal, though blind, developed compensatory abilities that can only be described as amazing. With its eyesight gone, the dog's ability to smell and to hear became super acute. Sporty would walk through the house and never collide with anything, even when the furniture was rearranged. A developed sensitivity to radar echoes or, perhaps, the smell of the furniture may have been the explanation.

"My uncle liked popcorn. Both the dog and I developed a taste for it, as well. After he went blind, Sporty would smell Uncle Calhoun's popcorn and sit beside him and beg. Uncle Calhoun would toss a kernel on the rug and Sporty's ears were so acute that he would locate and gobble it up before it stopped moving. Sporty was a superb example of how an intelligent animal can compensate for lost senses.

"One evening we were all eating popcorn while Uncle Calhoun showed me his coin collection. He handed me an 1893 San Francisco-minted dime. It was in excellent condition and was worth over five hundred dollars. That was a lot of money in 1939.

As I handed it back to him, the coin fell from my hand. No sooner had it hit the carpet than Sporty, thinking it was popcorn, found and swallowed it.

"I was devastated, but Uncle Calhoun remained calm. He went to the medicine cabinet and came back with a nearly full quart bottle of castor oil. I held Sporty's jaws open while my uncle forced the entire contents of the bottle down the animal's throat. Then, we locked poor Sporty in a small room in the basement.

"He was not a large dog. I didn't think his stomach could hold a quart of anything, let alone castor oil. I knew what a spoonful of the stuff did to me, and I feared for Sporty's well-being. He survived the evening, but I paid for my negligence. The next morning, I had to clean up that small room in the basement.

"I marveled at how such a small dog could produce so much by-product that, in its more liquid state, could cover so much floor space and so much of the walls and to such a high elevation." The Major again clinked the ice cubes in his again empty glass, signaling the end of the story.

One of the hunters asked the question that had occurred to everyone: "Did you find the dime?"

After a few second's pause, the Major said, "No. I didn't find it. You see, the coin was counterfeit, and the dog couldn't pass it."

Having diverted attention from the question of dog superiority, the Major led the way to the lodge dining room, where he and his friends enjoyed the evening meal.

14

HIGH CRIMES AND MISDEMEANORS

IN SEPTEMBER, THE EARTH CONTINUES ITS SLOW roll to one side, and the southern hemisphere begins to receive more hours of sunlight. As that roll continues, the days get shorter in the northern hemisphere, and the temperature begins to drop. The deciduous trees display their colors and prepare for snow. Those who have the wherewithal plan their annual southerly wintertime migration.

After Labor Day in northern Wisconsin, the summer people close their cottages and return to such beauty spots as Chicago, Milwaukee, or Racine. Many of them leave television sets, radios, and easily movable assets in their summer homes.

Those who don't close their cabins are hunters. They intend to use their places at least until the end of the deer season in late November. Their cottages might not contain television sets, but mounted heads and other such decorations, along with appliances needed to crush ice or mix drinks, will be found there.

When the autumn leaves begin to change color, thieves visit both the summer cottages and the cabins of hunters. They steal whatever can be easily transported. This is because the thieves are locals who, understandably, don't want to spend their winters in northern Wisconsin. They need money to finance travel to their winter nesting areas, commonly in Florida, Georgia, or Texas. So they steal from northern cottages and cabins, and peddle their loot in southern flea markets.

Major Nathaniel Peabody prefers a northern habitat during the months of October and November. Migratory waterfowl draw him to Minnesota, Michigan's Upper Peninsula, and Maine. Upland game calls him to Wisconsin.

Every year, a few days of the October or November pages of his kitchen wall calendar are overmarked with the words *Oconto County—ruffed grouse*. He goes to a cabin maintained by a shotgunning friend. It is one of the ones within the post-Labor Day route of a local thief. He breaks the window next to the door, enters, and commits his depredations.

The thief usually visits the cabin once every four years. He seems to think it takes four years for his victims to replace the stolen items and redevelop that sense of security essential to their feeling that it is okay to again leave the equipment in the cabin. Over the years, Major Peabody presented his friend with various artifacts intended to be hung on the cabin wall.

They included a pair of moose antlers (these were stolen four years later) and a set of handmade snowshoes found in a long-deserted northern Ontario village (these were stolen eight years later).

The Major often recalled those old, crude snowshoes and that set of moose antlers, and roundly damned the thief. He would castigate thieves, in general, and swear that if he ever caught the one who stole from his friend, "I would shoot him in an instant, and my conscience wouldn't bother me a whit."

If you overlook fraud involving less than a thousand dollars and various other misdemeanors, Major Peabody could be considered a law-abiding citizen. He has never been successfully prosecuted and convicted of committing a felony in this country. He has admitted that some unpleasantness did once occur in Venezuela, but that, he contends, doesn't count.

Peabody insists that he never cheats and always gives his intended victims a fair chance—or at least what appears to be a fair chance. Playing poker with him is an example. As I have already said, you may think you have a fair chance, but you rarely do.

I'm particularly sensitive to the twenty-dollar loss I suffered at the Major's hands when, as I have described, he put a cement building block on a stump and bet me he could shoot a .410 right through it. I've never really forgiven him for that wound, but a fair-minded observer would have to admit that he didn't actually cheat me. So, I guess he is within his rights to express indignation over the thievery of others.

But expressing indignation and suggesting murder are quite different matters. I was surprised to hear him threaten to kill the thief and assigned his comment to what may have been understandable hyperbole.

Last year, the Major took his annual fall ruffed-grouse trip to the Oconto County cabin of his hunting companion. It had been four years since the last theft, and the place was due for its quadrennial break-in. Peabody and his friends arrived there on a Friday afternoon. There was no sign of disturbance, and the Major was pleased to see that his last "wall gift," a large sulfur fungus he'd found in Minnesota, was still hanging in its accustomed place behind the potbellied stove.

That evening, the four hunters finished a trout dinner and actively engaged in finishing a liter of single-malt Scotch whisky. Someone suggested a pool be created for the next day's hunt. Everyone would contribute $25, to be given to the first one to bag a grouse or a woodcock. There would be another $25 for the hunter who bagged the most birds and still another $25 for the one who shot the last bird of the day.

The Major considered the hunting abilities of his three companions and calculated that he had an excellent chance to win at least two of the three pools. He didn't hesitate for a moment. Peabody was the first to accept the proposition.

The following morning, the weather was not favorable for the hunt. It was windy, and the birds were spooky. The dogs had difficulty finding a scent. Not a single grouse or woodcock was flushed.

The Major told me what happened then.

"I was in a foul mood. If I had shot but a single bird, I'd have taken seventy-five dollars from each of my three companions. Now I had to be content with nothing more than the return of my own seventy-five-dollar investment. When we got back to the cabin, I was the first one out of the truck. I took my Lefever out of its case and headed for the cabin to wipe off the drizzle and oil it for the next day.

"As I approached the cabin door, I saw that the adjacent window had been broken. I loaded the shotgun and carefully entered the building. I saw the culprit at the table. I shot him dead, dead, dead."

"Good God," I gasped, "you didn't."

"Oh, yes, I did," he answered. "Right there inside the cabin. The pellets that missed him punctured the stovepipe and ruined the sulfur fungus hanging on the wall behind it."

"What did you do with the body?" I asked.

"We ate him," said a smiling Major Peabody. "He was delicious. You see, a grouse had flown through the window and was sitting on the table. Of course, I had to shoot the vandal then and there. It meant two hundred and twenty-five dollars to me."

15

ERICKSON V. PEABODY

MAJOR NATHANIEL PEABODY, USA (RET.) was in northern Minnesota hunting ducks. He was staying at Keith Erickson's cabin on a marshy lake known to contain deepwater duck potato, sago pond plant, and wild rice. Though it was nearing the end of October, the lake also contained a goodly population of local puddle ducks.

I arrived in camp in the late afternoon. At the stroke of midnight, I would be authorized to give the Major his first-of-the-month spendthrift-trust remittance. Then I could drive to Bemidji and fly back to civilization.

The sun was down. Five of us were seated before a fieldstone fireplace watching three-foot logs burn and waiting for a wood duck, three mallards, two blue-winged teal and a lot of wild rice to bake in the oven of the woodstove. It smelled very good.

The conversation concerned the events of the day. Erickson had shared a blind with Major Peabody. He made a number of insulting remarks about the Major and told how a single wood duck, apparently with a strong death wish, had attempted to buzz their decoys. One loud boom was heard, and the duck had splashed down.

Major Peabody then took up the narrative. With highly disre-spectful and rude descriptions of Keith Erickson, he told how his claim of bagging the bird had been challenged. Through some sort of legerdemain, Erickson had been able to produce an empty 12-gauge shell from the chambers of his double. The Major had done the same. While they argued over who dropped the bird, Erickson's dog, a yellow Lab named Deuces Tecum, had sprung into the lake. As the dispute continued, the Lab had returned to the blind and dropped the wood duck at the Major's feet.

The other hunters settled the argument by declaring every yel-low Lab to be more trustworthy and honest than either of the two hunters. Since the dog brought the duck to the Major, they decided, it was his shot that killed the bird. Erickson was not happy with the finding. During the dinner, things turned ugly.

Erickson took a bite of the wood duck, uttered an expletive, and spit a pellet onto his plate. He immediately yelled out "Whiplash!" and began to moan and carry on in a distressful man-ner. This display continued unabated until Ole brought him a water glass half-filled with Uncle Jack.

Momentarily, at least, the medicine appeared to effectively ease his agony. Whenever the glass was empty, Erickson would moan a bit and rattle the ice. Ole would then provide an addi-tional dose.

After dinner, the pain having sufficiently subsided, Erickson cited the decision to award the kill to the Major. Then he accused Peabody of shooting in so negligent a manner as to leave a pellet in the edible portion of the duck. He demanded damages in the amount of one million dollars as compensation for pain and suf-fering and for the mental anguish he endured as a result of the fear that he may have damaged a molar.

Major Peabody vehemently denied each and every allegation of negligence. He lodged a cross-complaint, claiming Erickson's slanderous accusation held him up to public ridicule and contempt, injuring his well-established reputation as an expert shotgunner. Further, he demanded a million dollars as appropriate compensation. An immediate trial was insisted upon by both parties.

Because I was learned in matters of jurisprudence and the only attorney there, I was appointed judge. That's what I prefer to think. Ole claims I was appointed because everyone thought I was too innocent, credulous, and stupid to be crooked.

A jury was waived after it was learned (a) that one of the two potential jurors had solicited and accepted bribes from both contesting parties, and (b) the other candidate admitted to being a liberal. He was, thus, disqualified because Minnesota law specifically requires all jurors to be able to read and write. So, it was decided I should rule on matters both of law and fact, and the judicial proceedings began.

The plaintiff's testimony included Peabody's insistence that he shot the wood duck, the fact that Deuces Tecum brought the bird to him, and the finding by the other hunters that Peabody did, in fact, shoot the duck. Erickson entered an exhibit—the mangled pellet that had been fished out of the garbage. He asked me to take judicial notice of the torment and anguish he had shown during the meal.

To establish his defense, Peabody offered to provide the court with an affidavit from his Uncle Calhoun proving his peerless ability as a wingshot and establishing that he was not the kind of person who would consider allowing even a single pellet to hit the edible portion of a duck.

As an alternative defense, he testified that Erickson would look much better without teeth and, therefore, had suffered no damage. He also suggested the pellet may have been planted.

To confirm his contention of being a perfect shot, the Major called Deuces Tecum to the stand. Erickson objected. He claimed the Major had been giving the Lab doggie candy all day long and said it couldn't be believed. He muttered something about alienation of affection. He also argued that if a woman can't be forced to testify against her husband, surely a man's dog—much more loyal and friendly than a wife—should not be able to testify against him.

The objection was overruled. However, as the dog approached the witness box, it stopped, sniffed the leg of the judge's chair, and then performed an act that resulted in its being held in contempt of court. It was peremptorily ejected from the cabin before it could give any testimony.

Erickson's closing argument consisted of mentioning that the area had experienced an explosion in its bear population. All those beasts, he said, were hungry and particularly ferocious. Newspaper accounts of their attacking and eating wandering wayfarers were numerous. He wondered if I would be able to navigate the miles of serpentine logging roads lying between the cabin and the nearest county road. He concluded his argument by flatly stating that any judge who had the temerity to support the Major's case would be thrown out of the cabin in the middle of the night and be forced to find his way to town without benefit of auto, horse, mule, or lantern.

Major Peabody's closing argument consisted of two well-conceived arguments. First, he characterized the plaintiff's case as, "The absurd, fraudulent maundering of a man consumed with jealousy and fraught with vengeance for having been proven to have missed a shot." Second, he said that if I held in favor of Erickson, he would tell my fiancé, the lovely Stephanie (whom he referred to as "your ecologically sensitive, bird-loving paramour") that I was a man who, at the end of each month, surreptitiously traveled to out-of-the-way places where I secretly engaged in shotgunning and ruthlessly slaughtered her feathered friends.

My complete lack of any sense of direction and my well-known and inordinate panic at the mere thought of bear were equally balanced by my fear of the Major's ability to destroy my relationship with the lovely Stephanie.

Nevertheless, justice triumphed.

FINDINGS OF FACT AND CONCLUSIONS OF LAW

Major Nathaniel Peabody's reputation as a wingshooter who leaves no shot in the body of a bird is well established and must be recognized. On the other hand, there is no doubt that a pellet was inside the duck and that the plaintiff bit into it and spit it out on his plate.

The plaintiff's distress was apparent, and three heavy doses of medicine were required to alleviate his agony. He has, indeed, been damaged.

Major Peabody is usually of a phlegmatic nature. His

snorts, gasps, and obscene expressions of disbelief, voiced at various times during the plaintiff's testimony and argument, doubtlessly reflect his great anguish at being accused of malfeasance. If found guilty of negligently aiming, he, too, would be greatly damaged.

With potential claims for damages thus established, the question of just who is responsible must be addressed.

It is clear to the court that the wood duck in question must have been shot last year, surviving until this season with a single pellet in its chest. By the judgment of this court, the Major's reputation remains unblemished, and it is unnecessary to award damages to him.

With Major Peabody freed from any negligence, the plaintiff's claim for damages cannot stand. The plaintiff must seek out and sue the hunter who, last year, made the improper shot.

Both cases were dismissed with prejudice, and peace and tranquillity prevailed.

16

THE SECRET PLACE

FREDDIE FISCHER ISN'T COMFORTABLE WHENEVER he is in a city with a population in excess of 5,000. Still, every Labor Day weekend, Freddie leaves his home in the Maine woods and drives his wife, one of the Larson girls, to Philadelphia for the annual family reunion.

Freddie's opinion of the quality of life in that city is best summed up by his observation that the airplanes arriving in Philadelphia are nearly always empty but that the airplanes leaving Philadelphia are nearly always filled to capacity.

The trip is made bearable only because it gives Freddie an opportunity to visit with his hunting buddy, Major Nathaniel Peabody, and talk about ruffed grouse. When the bird season opens, the Major and Doc Carmichael are often found in Freddie's northern Maine camp. Freddie and the Major are good friends.

On the morning of the Larson's most recent Philadelphia assembly, as was his well-established custom, Freddie deposited Jessie at the clan headquarters, quickly excused himself, and headed for the Major's apartment. Major Peabody had offered him sanctuary. and Freddie planned to spend the entire day with him.

Age does take its toll, and the Major was no spring chicken, but Freddie was shocked by his appearance on this occasion. Peabody always greeted his old friend with an *abrazo*. Now he was unable to do so. When Freddie came into the apartment, he saw the Major clutching an aluminum-tubed walker in both hands.

Major Peabody's shoulders were bent forward, as was his head, denying the military bearing that he had always maintained. There was no impish sparkle in his eyes. No ebullient grin covered his face. And as he transferred himself from the walker to his favorite wing-backed chair, Freddie noticed a slight tremor in his hand and watched that insecurity of movement sometimes found in the very old.

"It must have been a stroke," Freddie thought, and he wondered why no one had told him about it. Certainly Peabody had aged substantially since he last saw him less than a year ago. The Major seemed so old. Somehow it never occurred to Freddie that Nathaniel Peabody would ever be old.

"Freddie, Freddie," greeted the Major. "How marvelous to see you again. (Pause) I suppose you've heard. Well, I guess I'm adjusting. (Pause) I'm so glad, so glad you came," he said, showing sincere affection for his hunting companion.

Peabody's physical deterioration was bad enough. The real tragedy was the fact that his mind was not affected by the stroke. From his conversation, Freddie knew the Major had not lost his active interest in shotgunning. That interest, coupled with his inability to participate in the hunt, had to be a torment to him.

While the Major appeared to have some control of his body, clearly his muscular system was impaired. He was weak. Hence the walker. And hence the Major's embarrassment when he admitted he couldn't even open a bottle of scotch. He hadn't had a drink in four days. Freddie corrected that situation forthwith by uncorking a bottle.

It was distressing to Freddie to suddenly realize that Major Peabody made no reference to future plans. Usually he spoke of coming trips to shoot *perdiz* in Argentina or goose in Canada or whitewings in Honduras. Now he spoke only of the past—and mostly about ruffed-grouse hunts with Freddie in northern Maine. "Remember whens" salted their conversation.

"Major, I'll never forget your story about the time you shot the grouse that flew in through the window of the Wisconsin cabin."

"Yes, Freddie. And remember last year? We hunted all day long and had only one bird for dinner. Then you went out, all by yourself, and got three more in less than forty-five minutes."

"I sure do remember, Major. And I remember when you stole Doc Carmichael's shells and replaced them with the ones you'd filled with sugar sand."

Matters got serious later in the day when Freddie came back from a trip to get Chinese take-out food and a few fifths of single-malt Scotch whisky to resupply the Major's now substantially damaged stockpile of same. After Freddie carefully uncorked all three new bottles and put them in Peabody's liquor cabinet, the Major confided that he intended to keep his 20-gauge Lefever double barrel with him as a remembrance of things past but had arranged to bequeath it to Freddie for "when the time comes."

This was nearly too much for Freddie. He turned his back to Peabody and had to blink a few times to keep tears from forming. He quickly changed the subject, and the two old friends shared secrets and memories of happier times.

It was two in the morning when Major Peabody poured Freddie Fischer into a cab, instructing the driver to deposit him at the Robert Morris Hotel.

The next morning, Doc Carmichael received a telephone call.

"Doc? This is Peabody. Freddie came in yesterday morning. We got plastered. I sat in the easy chair, and he brought me drinks all day long. It worked pretty much as I thought it would. It took a long time but, after a considerable depletion of my stock of whisky and a promise to leave my Lefever to him, he finally broke down and told me where he shot those three grouse last fall.

"You go out to the end of Old Shingle Mill Road and then head northwest for about a quarter-mile. Freddie found a field next to a cedar swamp on Consolidated Paper land. He's been seeding it with clover for years. Towards evening and early in the morning, every ruffed grouse in Blaine County feeds on that clover.

"We can drive up on Friday afternoon and be on Old Shingle Mill Road when the season opens on Saturday. I suspect Freddie will hunt there, too. It's his secret place. I look forward to seeing his expression when we meet. You might prepare some kind of 'miraculous cure' explanation for him. And come pick up this silly walker. I damn near fell over it three times. Bring a couple of bottle of single-malt to replace the ones Freddie drank."

On his way back to Maine, Freddie Fischer was in a pensive mood. He was truly shocked by the Major's condition. He'd have to remember to call Doc Carmichael and see if it would be possible to bring Peabody into camp near the end of the season—to be there to enjoy the surroundings, even though he wouldn't be able to get out and hunt.

As he reviewed the previous day's happenings, Freddie thought, "Perhaps I shouldn't have lied to the Major when he asked me about the location of my clover field. Oh, well, he'll never hunt grouse again anyway, so I didn't do any damage."

17

How to Succeed Without Really Trying

MAJOR PEABODY RETURNED from a duck hunt in Saskatchewan in such a weakened financial condition that I couldn't help but provide im with a loan for basic necessities. It would be another two weeks before he would receive his monthly remittances.

Now, only two days later, I was putting his duffel bag and leg 'mutton shotgun case into the back seat of my car. He had asked me to take him to the airport to catch a flight to Central America. He was going on another duck-hunting trip.

Of course, I was curious. Where had he gotten the money? A broadly smiling Major Peabody recognized my curiosity but limited himself to a single comment: "Bread upon the water, my boy. Bread upon the water."

Whenever I hinted about the source of his funding, he would change the subject. It was frustrating for me, and he knew it. As we drove toward the aiport, the Major asked, "Did I ever tell you how I achieved my captaincy?"

Knowing that my questions about his financial state would go unanswered, I replied, "No," whereupon he proceeded with his tale.

World War II had ended. Peabody was a first lieutenant and had finished his tour of duty in Colombia and was assigned to a United States embassy located in Central America. His host country was ruled by a tin-pot dictator named Chavez. Chavez's private sympathies had been with the Axis, but now he posed no serious threat to anyone other than his countrymen.

All in all, Lieutenant Peabody's life at his new post was free from stress. It was his custom to devote Mondays, Tuesdays, and Wednesdays to performing his duties as the embassy's military attaché. On those days, he would prepare and give his reports to the ambassador. They covered the strength of the republic's armed forces, the personalities of its generals, and gossip gleaned from the attachés of other embassies. Some of Peabody's reports were factual.

For the balance of the week, Lieutenant Peabody "investigated matters military." He did so with Capitan Francisco "Pancho" Fuentes and his friends, Antonio Gonzalez and Alberto Vargas. Pancho Fuentes was the son of the country's largest rice producer. Rice fields attract ducks. Rice growers look upon ducks as pests, and—it must be admitted—ducks do enjoy eating rice.

At an early age, Pancho was given a scattergun and asked to help reduce the population of those flying vandals. And Pancho found an avocation. Young Fuentes had no interest in growing rice—or in any part of the business world for that matter. So, he became an officer in the army. It was a respectable position for the son of a wealthy rice grower.

Pancho's interest in pass-shooting was shared by Antonio

Gonzalez, a local *medico*, and by Alberto Vargas, a professor at the University of San Simon. In his college days, Professor Vargas had been a member of his country's rifle team and, as such, he had represented the nation in the Pan American Games. That representation later caused him discomfort and anxiety.

President Chavez was an old-fashioned dictator. Rather than run any risk of facing an armed popular revolt, he imposed strict gun-control laws. The rules for importing weapons were particularly stringent. If it became known that a citizen owned a gun, his name was put on "The List." Whenever there was a suggestion of political unrest, everyone on The List was rounded up and put in jail until things quieted down. The local jails were built in the last century and, it is rumored, were modeled after those used in the Spanish Inquisition.

Languishing in one of them for even a few days was, as Professor Vargas reported, a memorable experience. After he had been interned because of his ownership of a Pan American Games team rifle, he turned the weapon over to the government and had his name removed from The List. The government never found out about his shotgun.

As an army officer, Fuentes ran no risk insofar as a revolver and rifle were concerned. They were government issue. But he never admitted that he privately owned a duck gun. Doctor Gonzalez had also been able to hide his ownership of a shotgun. For years, Fuentes, Vargas, and Gonzalez hunted together, but none of them wanted to fight the red tape or undergo the scrutiny involved in trying to import a new shotgun. And, at times, they had difficulty finding shells.

Of course, all three men knew that Lieutenant Peabody was

attached to the United States Embassy and enjoyed diplomatic immunity. Among other advantages, diplomatic immunity meant that Peabody could receive weapons and ammunition in diplomatic shipments that were not subject to review by customs officials.

There are those who contend his diplomatic immunity was the reason Peabody was able to become one of the regulars in that closely knit hunting group. Regardless, Fuentes, Gonzalez, Vargas, and Peabody traveled all over the republic hunting duck and dove and pigeon.

During these outings. Peabody learned of the difficulties involved in bringing a shotgun into the country. Professor Vargas told the lieutenant of his gun-related incarcerations. Peabody saw how his companions nearly salivated as they touched and admired his Fox double. He noticed the shabby condition of their own armament.

Of course, Peabody knew he could arrange to quietly get weapons into the republic. He offered to do so, and his friends were delighted. They carefully selected the weapons they wanted, and shortly thereafter, three high-quality shotguns were delivered to the embassy. They were passed on to the hunters without a paper trail.

One morning, while they all shared a duck blind, Professor Vargas explained a problem he faced. He was responsible for training his republic's Pan American Games rifle team. They needed twenty target rifles. But if the students were successful in getting importation permits, their names would be added to The List. No student would become a member of the rifle team if his name were placed on Presidente Chavez's list.

Peabody recognized the professor's explanation of the rifle

team's problem as an indirect request for help. He didn't hesitate. The lieutenant picked up an embassy form and requisitioned twenty rifles. He gave it to the professor to identify the manufacturer, specify the proper caliber, and order an appropriate quantity of ammunition. The requisition went to Washington, and Peabody's popularity soared with all three friends.

A month later, Lieutenant Peabody's serene and pleasant existence took a turn for the worse. His troubles began on Wednesday. That was the day Capitan Francisco "Pancho" Fuentes called and canceled their Thursday duck hunt. He also canceled the Friday, Saturday, and Sunday duck hunts.

Fuentes offered no explanation. He didn't even talk with Peabody. He left a brief note saying that he and his friends would be "busy." Peabody knew he must have offended them, but he had no idea what he had done. To have his friends suddenly cancel the hunts, without any kind of explanation was a serious disappointment.

On Thursday things got worse. The American ambassador told Peabody to immediately pack up and return to Washington D.C. There he was to be questioned about irregularities in his requisitions. And on Friday afternoon things got still worse. Peabody was in the Pentagon, standing at rigid attention before a scowling and very unhappy Major General Peter Atkinson.

"If it weren't for your family name, Peabody," said the general in what came very close to being a growl, "you would be peremptorily cashiered. Involving yourself in the importation of weapons while serving as a military attaché is unthinkable. If you have an explanation, give it to me now."

"Yes, sir," said Peabody. "You are acquainted with the near

impossibility of importing arms into that country. I signed documents to arrange the silent delivery of a few shotguns for friends and twenty rifles for the university rifle squad. That squad will represent the country in the next Pan Am Games. While the procedure may not have been strictly according to drill, I hope the general will consider support for the country's rifle team to outweigh any modest irregularities. Public relations and a gesture of good will—"

Peabody got no farther.

"Lieutenant Peabody," growled the major general, "you may try to convince me you signed an order for a few weapons. But you won't be successful. Look at this." He handed Peabody the requisition he had signed and forwarded a month earlier. It called for the delivery of 2,000 rifles. Someone had added two zeros to the order.

While Peabody stared at the amended requisition, General Atkinson growled again: "I'll expect you to personally give me your written resignation from the service on Monday morning at 10 A.M. That is all. Now get out of here."

We were nearing the airport, and Major Peabody hurried to finish the story.

"No, young man," he said to me. "It had not been a good week for me. But things brightened up on Monday. With signed resignation in hand, I arrived at General Atkinson's office precisely at the appointed hour. The general was unexpectedly cordial. He met me at his office door, smiled, extended his hand, and said, 'Well, Nathaniel, did you have a pleasant weekend? Sit down, sit down. We're very informal here. Would you like a cigar? I get some from Havana in every diplomatic pouch that comes up.'

"I thought the old boy must have gone mad.

" 'Sorry about that little mix-up on Friday,' he said. 'I just got a full report from the ambassador. I guess we finally got rid of that damned old Nazi, Chavez. When he saw 2,000 armed people marching on the governmental palace, he caved in, managed to get to the airport, and flew to Spain.' "

Peabody shook his head as we pulled into the airport. "Then I knew why Vargas had been so friendly," he said to me. "General Atkinson confirmed my suspicions when he told me that a university professor, a young army captain, and a medical doctor had formed a junta that was ruling the country. General Atkinson must have thought I was in on it.

"He lit a match, held it to my cigar, and said, 'Brilliant work, Nathaniel, brilliant work. The guys at the CIA are livid. The good old army stole a march on them, eh? Of course, we can't send you back there. But, there's some great dove hunting in Honduras, and I can arrange a post for you at Tegucigalpa. You'll get your captaincy just as soon as I can press the right buttons.' "

I carried the Major's bag to the check-in. "That's how you became a captain?" I asked.

"Yes, my boy, that's how it happened. And to satisfy your youthful curiosity, that's also how it is that I'm flying to Central America. We're all getting a bit older, and former president Vargas has invited me back. He, General Fuentes, and I are having a reunion. We'll hunt ducks for a week—this time at their goverment's expense."

18

THE MAJOR AND THE STOCK MARKET

"IT'S ALL YOUR FAULT, YOU KNOW," said Major Nathaniel Peabody, as he helped himself to a cigar from the humidor on a shelf of my bookcase. The Major gave me the expensive humidor. He knows I don't smoke, but he advised me of my responsibility to never allow the humidor to be completely void of content. The gift of the humidor serves the purpose of assuring him of smoking material whenever he visits my apartment.

Then he poured more than a dollop of Famous Grouse into a water glass and added ice cubes. "I prefer The Glenlivet," he said as he sat in my favorite chair next to the fireplace.

"What's all my fault?" I inquired, knowing immediately that I shouldn't have asked the question.

"On the first day of every month," the Major answered, "you hand me my monthly ration of money. And at least once a month, you provide me with a lecture about the manner in which I manage my funds. My common end-of-month condition, you claim, could be alleviated by a savings and investment program.

"I've resisted your Siren's song because all of my natural

instincts rebel against the theory that money should be stacked up in neat piles and stuffed into a mattress or given to a banker. Money was made to be used. It should be expended for the pleasure and benefit of its temporary owner.

"Savings accounts and investments, young man," he continued, "destroy the purpose of money. Moreover, they make one greedy. And, were I to embark upon such a program, I would have to manage and watch over it. It would steal my time. And it would destroy the priorities of my life—priorities I've developed over years of admirable profligacy."

"But, Major," I protested, "just a modicum of planning would eliminate your unfortunate end-of-month pattern. Here it is, a week before the day I can deliver your check, and I suspect that you are without a penny to your name."

"Not so. Not so", he answered. "I have a handful of change. But I would have adequate funds if I hadn't fallen prey to the false logic of your arguments."

I freshened his glass with more Famous Grouse. (My supply of The Glenlivet was now hidden on the top shelf of my closet.) Then I asked him to tell me, in plain English and without embellishment, the reason why he accused me of causing his current impecunious condition.

"In plain English and without embellishment . . ." he repeated. "I am somewhat pained by your implied suggestion that I might present facts in other than my usual straightforward manner, but I will overlook it," he said, neglecting to acknowledge my look of disbelief.

"Some two months ago, after buying my usual first-of-the month supplies—refreshment, shells, orange juice, and bread—I gave serious thought to your insistence that I set aside some monies for investment. On the spur of the moment. I decided to take your advice. I bought a lottery scratch card and won two hundred dollars!

"I was overjoyed and, frankly, quite impressed with this 'investment business.' Then and there I reconsidered my previous negative reactions to your various money management lectures. The vision of investing in order to produce the money needed to pay for longer and more distant hunting forays appeared before me. Like some terrible disease, the investment germ had entered my system.

"The following week, I hunted quail in North Carolina with Benjamin Rusk. You might know him. He's president of the Corn Exchange Bank. He has the reputation of being a particularly shrewd investor. Watching him, I thought, 'If anyone who shoots as badly as he does can make a fortune in the investment business, so can I.' I paid close attention to what he said. After dinner he advised me to buy stock in a company called Mineria Durango y Chihuahua. He confided that the company was a Mexican mining venture with a past lackluster performance. However, its copper mines contained recently discovered, but not yet publicly reported, veins of gold. The stock would soon skyrocket.

"Back in Philadelphia, I found that the stock was traded on the Denver Exchange and cost fifteen cents a share. I took my two-hundred-dollar nest egg, added other funds to it, and bought 2,000 shares. Within a month, Mineria Durango y Chihuahua stock was selling for three dollars a share. I could cash in and more than cover the costs of an Argentina waterfowl, perdiz, and snipe hunt. But if I hung on, I reasoned, the way this investment business works, I'd be able to afford to go there and to Tanzania.

"Two days ago, when I returned from Saskatchewan, I called my broker to determine how many shares I needed to sell to pay for my Argentine and African adventures. You are unable to imagine the extent of my surprise when he told me Mineria Durango y Chihuahua stock was worthless. The gold vein report was only a rumor. It had no basis in fact. The Mexican company officers, who owned the great majority of the stock, sold out when it reached three dollars and fifty cents a share. They all resigned their posts and are now living in Brazil.

"I called Benjy at his office in the Corn Exchange Bank to inquire about the stock. His only comment was, 'Oh, do you still own that stock?'

"Now then, counselor," the Major said to me, "this is all your fault. My sympathies have never been with the ants. They have always been with the grasshoppers. Aesop—and you—should have minded your own business.

"You must bear responsibility for the 'saving-for-a-rainy-day' philosophy you foisted upon me. I hold you personally liable for my loss. Let's see . . . 2,000 shares times $3.50. That's seven thousand dollars."

What could I do. After convincing the Major his loss was really limited to his out-of-pocket expenses, I gave him $350 and promised to make no further suggestion about the way he (mis)managed his money.

A few days later I met Benjamin Rusk, the president of the Corn Exchange Bank, at a cocktail party. I asked him why he hadn't given Major Peabody timely advice on selling the Mineria Durango y Chihuahua stock. Benjy told me:

1) He did not know and had never met anyone named Nathaniel Peabody,

2) He had never heard of a stock called Mineria Durango y Chihuahua, and,

3) He had never hunted in his life.

19

CARPE DIEM

MAJOR NATHANIEL PEABODY, USA (ret.) has no one to blame but himself. His guaranteed monthly stipends would allow most of us to live quite comfortably and set aside a tidy bit for a rainy day.

But not so with the Major. Oh, no. If you mention "rainy day" to Peabody, he immediately thinks of duck hunting. The Major is well aware of the amount of his income. He knows the costs of his hunting forays. He knows he contracts to spend more on hunting than the total amount of his income. And he does it again and again and again. The why of it all is a puzzle to me.

Major Peabody's management of his finances has been characterized as "The Horse Trader Syndrome": The buyer purchases the horse and returns it the next day. He says the first time he hitched the horse to his buggy, it ran off the road and into a field of standing corn. The buyer claims the horse is blind in one eye and demands his money back. The horse trader refuses, saying, "Hell, that horse ain't blind. He just don't give a damn."

Financial insecurity doesn't bother the Major. He just doesn't seem to give a damn.

I suspect he enjoys having to live by his wits for a few days every month. And he has never, never violated his own rule against engaging in what he refers to as "that most degrading practice of seeking a loan."

I'm sure Major Peabody looks upon the solving of his temporary financial problems as a game. And it is a game he plays very well. Let me give you an example. One fall, the Major was in the Maine woods chasing woodcock. He was with four other hunters.

The host of the woodcock hunt was Pete Scheinert, a logger and mill owner. Pete had retired, and his sons were managing the business. ("So well," reported Pete, "that I can hunt and fish whenever and wherever I like, and never have to worry about the corporation.") Pete and his company owned a lot of Maine woodlands.

Another companion, Charlie Johnson, enjoyed a less affluent existence. He left school when in the sixth grade in order to work in the woods and help support the family, money being a very scarce commodity in the 1930s. By the time World War II improved the economy, Charlie had developed a great love for the woods and refused all offers of better-paying jobs in town.

Charlie worked for Pete for many years. He was much more than merely an employee. He was Pete's guide and hunting companion and friend. They had a lot in common—except that Charlie drank an awful lot more than Pete.

Jerry Heinz was the third member of the team. He was an auto dealer. He had a big operation in Milwaukee and sold a lot of cars. He played a passable game of gin rummy and was known to wager a bit on the card games. Jerry was a likeable cuss. The Major once said, publicly, "I'd buy a used car from that man."

Doc Hostetler completed the company. He started his career as a New England general practitioner. He ended up with a clinic bearing his name and containing a number of capable medicos and administrators. He had the reputation of being a shrewd operator—like the Connecticut Yankees of old.

As was his usual practice when hunting with strangers for the first time, Major Peabody carefully surveyed his companions to determine which might be the most productive in the event additional funds were needed to cover expenses during the last part of the month. Obviously, Charlie Johnson was out of the running. His financial structure was one that the Major would not attack. Likewise, Pete Scheinert was eliminated as a prospect. It's not polite to take advantage of the host, especially when he has access to a lot of hunting territory. He might be the source of future invitations to hunt grouse in prime bird habitat.

While Heinz's penchant for gin rummy appeared to be an open source of financial assistance—nearly as reliable as a federal-government program—the Major preferred to direct his attentions to Doc Hostetler. Outsmarting a shrewd New Englander was more appealing than getting ahead of a mid-western auto dealer—in spite of their reputation for always coming out on top of the deal. But trapping Doc Hostetler turned out to be no easy task.

Major Peabody purposely missed easy shots while standing next to him. He also managed to lose two dollars to Jerry at the gin table in the doctor's presence. Three days went by, and Hostetler never rose to any of the bait the Major scattered before him. He displayed no evidence of the greed or curiosity that usually motivate people to wager.

The Major had resigned himself to the slow process of securing his additional financial resources from Jerry Heinz. Then Charlie Johnson came to the rescue. Charlie had been dipping into Jerry's supply of George Dickel. He had also taken liberal samples of Doc Hostetler's favored Canadian rye. In order not to discriminate, Charlie had also tested the Major's bottle of The Glenlivet.

Charlie reported that the scotch at the top of the bottle tasted good. He later reported the scotch at the center of the bottle also tasted good.

It was nearly midnight when Charlie's yell, followed by cursing, roused the other hunters. Charlie had decided the fireplace needed more wood. He'd taken the two-bitted ax to split some beech that had been aging behind the cabin for a full season.

Charlie claimed the accident was due to the lack of moonlight. Pete claimed it was due too much moonshine. In any event, Charlie had missed the block of beech and opened up a dreadful gash in his foot. He was carried into the cabin and laid on the kitchen table. Then Doc Hostetler went into action.

He cut off the pants leg, exposing the bottoms of Charlie's heavy long johns. The term "unclean," when applied to those long-john bottoms, was an Olympic-sized understatement. Then Doc cut the bootlaces and, accompanied by a chorus of yells and curses from Charlie, he removed the boot. Instantly all of the other hunters wrinkled their noses and involuntarily stepped back a full pace. The offensive effluvia that assailed them from the foot were nearly overpowering.

Charlie's lifestyle had been such that he first became acquainted with plumbing while in his teens. At that time some of the people who lived in the woods were still being sewn into their winter underwear in the fall—there to remain until the spring thaw. (The trapdoors in the underwear were not sewn shut.)

Charlie lived in the woods. With no wife to bother him, he sometimes went for two or three months without a bath or a change of socks. And this was one of the "three-month" periods.

The Doc was up to it. He cut off the filthy stocking and applied some disinfectant—to the foot, not the stocking. Charlie said, "Ouch!" (and then he said some other words).

Doc Hostetler said: "Get me that leather awl and the boiled thread. I've never seen a foot this dirty in my entire practice." Then he began to stitch up the wound. Charlie said, "Ouch!" (and then he said some other words).

The Doc said: "Even the feet of the Australian aborigines are cleaner. They occasionally get rained on."

Charlie said: "Ouch" (and then he said some other words). It was then that the Doc made his mistake.

He said: "I'll bet a hundred dollars I'll never again see a foot this dirty."

There was a pause and Major Nathaniel Peabody said quietly, "You've got a bet, Doc."

Doc Hostetler put down the awl and contemplated the Major. He knew Peabody was not known to make rash wagers. He said: "Nat, I believe you're going to have trouble with this bet. Just how are you going to prove that I may, at some future date, see another foot this dirty?"

"That's easy, Doc," answered the Major. And he began to unlace Charlie's other boot.

20

TOMATO JUICE

IT WAS A THURSDAY MORNING AND THE END of the month. Major Nathaniel Peabody was hunting woodcock in Maine. I had to leave Philadelphia that same afternoon in order to deliver his check. I was in a bad mood, fighting a deadline, and over my ears in work.

While preparing a brief in support of a motion for a summary judgment dismissing a lawsuit against one of Smythe, Hauser, Engels & Tauchen's favorite clients, and in spite of clear instructions that I was not to be disturbed for any reason short of news of an impending collision of the planets, the intercom buzzed.

My secretary informed me, "Major Peabody is on the line and tells me if I don't let him talk to you immediately he will put me under a spell that will turn my hair undyeably gray." She sounded frightened and, I'm sure, was convinced the Major would actually do it.

"Thank you, Charlotte. Put him on."

"Hello, Major. How are things in Maine?" I inquired. Then a disquieting thought occurred. "You are in Maine, aren't you?" I added. I had visions of being informed that he was in Paraguay or Africa and of being advised to deliver his monthly stipend to Concepción or to some veldt camp in Zimbabwe.

I was relieved when the Major said, "Of course I'm in Maine. And we've been very lucky. The woodcock migration is underway, and the bird population is excellent." He paused for a second, but before I could interject a comment, he added, in a somewhat more somber tone, "With the exception of a fairly serious problem with a skunk, it has been one of the best outings I've had in years."

Although I'm a city boy, I know about skunks. Even before I met the Major, I knew they smelled bad, and now I know they can aim and shoot. I learned that four years earlier when I brought the Major's monthly trust installment check to the very same Maine hunting cabin he now occupied.

I recall the details of the encounter and its *sequelae* with perfect clarity. I had to bury my clothing. The next day, I drove the rental automobile back to Presque Isle while wearing some of the Major's old clothes. But the aroma of skunk lingered on. At the airport, the Hertz people were extremely unhappy. I had plenty of room on the flight back to Philadelphia. Four people changed their seats in order to get away from me.

The unfortunate experience with that striped animal left an indelible impression, and I subsequently made an impromptu study of it. One of the facts reported about skunks continues to fascinate me. It is said they won't "go off" if you grab them by the tail and quickly lift them into the air. I wonder who was the first man to perform that heroic act. I wonder if anyone else has ever had the courage to attempt it.

All of these thoughts ran through my mind when the Major mentioned the problem with the skunk. "Into each life, some rain must fall, Major," I told him. "I expect you may want me to bring some tomato juice with me?" It was a question, but I was sure of the answer.

"This is amazing," he said, "You've read my mind. That is the exact reason for my call. Bring a case of tomato juice with you. I look forward to seeing you, my boy," and he hung up.

Though my encounter with the skunk occurred two years ago, I still remembered the abuse I received from Major Peabody and his companion hunters. From a safe distance, they threw insulting comments at me. They gleefully heaped them atop the injuries I had suffered from the skunk's noxious spray.

After I dug the hole and buried my clothing, I stood naked outside the cabin and was subjected to a number of indelicate remarks until the Major tossed old boots, pants, and a wool shirt at me. I had to eat dinner outside in the dark and spend the night in the cold, open back of a pickup truck. I didn't sleep much for fear of bear. They all called me "Downwind."

But now my workload seemed to lighten, and my whole outlook on life improved as the old adages came to mind: "It's a long road that doesn't have a turn in it." "The shoe is on the other foot." "As ye give, so shall ye receive." I looked forward to the trip to Maine. It would be payback time. Oh, how they all were going to get it.

I drove an Avis rental car from the Presque Isle airport. (The woman at the Hertz desk remembered the skunk episode and refused my business.) During the two-hour trip to the woodcock cabin, various witty and stinging comments were created and memorized, e.g., "I must comment on the deterioration of the standards maintained by your local skunks. Two years ago they sought out only the best and the brightest for their special attentions. Now it appears humans who are far below them in social and intellectual rank are acceptable associates." And, e.g., "I'm sorry if you are offended by my insistence on the truth, but you smell much better now than you did before the skunk sprayed you."

It was already dark when I approached the two-rut road that led from the graveled county highway to the cabin occupied by Major Peabody and his friends. As I made the turn, I was glad to see the red glow of a cigar. It meant the Major was there, waiting to lead me through the maze of logging trails to the cabin.

"Glad to see you, my boy," he offered as he came up to the car. "You've brought the tomato juice?" Before I could insist he ride the hood of the vehicle rather than enter and permanently contaminate it, he was on the seat beside me. To my chagrin, he didn't smell of skunk. Oh well, I would direct my clever, pointed quips at someone else.

Major Peabody didn't mention skunk on the ride to the cabin. I brought up the subject and asked him what had happened. "Oh, that" he said. "It was two nights ago. We had steaks, and Charlie did the dishes. You know Charlie. He is not always Ph.D. material. When it came time to clean the skillet, he took it outside and poured out the grease, not too far from the door.

"At two in the morning, a poker game was in progress, and nature called. Charlie went outside and, as he walked toward the outhouse he almost tripped over the skunk that was licking up the grease. It came as a surprise to both of them. The skunk fired without properly aiming just as Charlie leaped out of the way.

"The serious nature of the occurrence is obvious when you recall there is only one door in the cabin—and that one was blocked by the odious calling card of the skunk. Well, Charlie found a ladder and leaned it up against the back window. We have to use it to come and go. It's a bit inconvenient, but by next spring it will be safe to use the door again."

Sorely disappointed by this account, I said, "Then you want

the tomato juice to soak the area that was sprayed by the skunk?"

"Heavens no," he answered. "The hunting is so good we're going to spend three more days here. We ran out of tomato juice and need more for the Bloody Marys."

Carrying the case of tomato juice, I followed the Major up the ladder. When I stuck my head into the building, Charlie looked up and said, "Well, if it isn't Downwind."

And it started all over again.

21

THE EYE OF THE BEHOLDER

Instead of dirt and poison, we have rather chosen to fill our lives with honey and wax, thus furnishing mankind with the two noblest of things, which are sweetness and light.

Jonathan Swift
A Tale of a Tub

MAJOR NATHANIEL PEABODY LOOKED OUT the window of his Philadelphia apartment at a late-January scene. The temperature was in the mid-thirties. As the snow melted, the debris that had accumulated on it during December and early January did not melt. The dust and dirt and soot remained on top of the banks, changing the snow's color from white to a dingy, brown gray. It was a somber and pessimistic scene.

Though dirt won't melt or evaporate, some of it floated down with the melting snow that formed growing puddles of slush. A sheet of muddy water covered the streets and sidewalks. Whenever a taxi driver saw an opportunity to speed past a pedestrian and pay his special respects, the splashed mud and water and slush would cover heavy winter coats and provide income for dry cleaners.

The mud and the water and the slush would also be tracked inside the building where the Major maintained his living quarters. The super wouldn't clean the rugs until spring. Major Peabody was convinced that at least half the dirt tracked into the apartment building ended up on his own carpet.

It was the Major's practice to buy a throw rug every December. He'd put it at the inside entranceway to his apartment. There it would collect most of the mud and slush from his shoes. The little rug would remain untouched until May. Then Major Peabody would pick it up, being careful not to disturb the then deeply encrusted dirt, and throw the whole thing away. "That's why they called it a 'throw rug,' " he once explained to me.

With the regularity of the geese flying south in the autumn, Major Peabody flew somewhere to hunt in a more temperate climate every January. Viewing the scene from his window, he was happy that the date of his annual January escape was approaching. He had already absorbed too much of Philadelphia's gray brown, grimy January.

The time had come for him to pick up the shotgun and take to the field. As was his custom, Major Peabody asked me to drive him to the airport. I looked forward to the Major's midwinter trip. It often meant he would be in a warm country at the end of the month. Then I, too, could escape the cold and the dirt when I traveled there to give him his first-of-the-month retirement and spendthrift-trust remittances.

So I was happily at his apartment, ready to do his bidding. As I carried the leg-o'-mutton shotgun case and duffel bag from the building to my automobile, I noticed the throw rug at the inside entranceway. The month wasn't even February, and yet the carpet was already filthy. I didn't think it would last until May.

On the way to the airport, Major Peabody confided: "January is one of those very long months. It contains thirty-one days—thirty-one days of mud and dirt. February is also a tough month to be in Philadelphia. But it has the courtesy to contain only twenty-eight days." Then he added, "Occasionally it gets obstreperous and squeezes in another one."

Major Peabody was on his way to Nicaragua on a humanitarian mission. At least, that's what he called it. He claimed that the Nicaraguan blue-winged teal population had exploded and was eating so much of the sesame seed and rice crop that it was threatening the economy of the country's northwestern provinces. He and three of his friends had volunteered to go there and help to resolve the problem.

As we approached the airport, Peabody's spirits rose. "To spend an entire winter covered in the grime and mud of this drab city requires an ability I've never been able to develop," he said. Then, after a pause, he looked at me with his Cheshire-cat grin and added: "I envy you, my boy. I'm so sorry I'm not a successful lawyer. Then I'd be able to stay here in Philadelphia tending to my clients' businesses and enjoying this weather."

*   *   *

After their weapons and luggage passed through the customs routine in Managua, the Major and his friends got into a Suburban for the drive to Arbol Viejo, the *finca* that would be their home for the next week. The vehicle left the road on the many occasions when the potholes represented a danger even their fearless driver considered to be too great a challenge.

It was the dry season. Off the highway, clouds of dust came up from around the Suburban's tires as they rolled over the dry ground. But there was plenty of water in the lake the men would hunt. It was a dusty, two-hour ride and, without complaint, the hunters arrived at Arbol Viejo where showers and dinner awaited them.

The next morning, long before sunrise, a knock on the door announced it was time for breakfast and then the drive to Lago Playita, the local headquarters of the sesame/rice eating bandit ducks. The hunters arrived at the lake before dawn. Duck blinds with shooting platforms had been built on stilts and sat some three feet above the water. There were four hunters. There were three blinds.

The Major drew the short straw. He would have to stand waist deep in the water's heavy marine vegetation. But the water was warm. It was shirtsleeve hunting, and the lack of cover didn't discourage the teal from flying well within the range of his gun.

At eleven o'clock, the airboat picked up the four men and their guides. By that time, most of Peabody's companions had gone through one of the cases of shells each had been provided, and they were ready for lunch and a siesta.

And by that time, the Major's feet had sunk so deeply into the muddy bottom of the lake he needed assistance and had to be pulled loose. He looked forward to an afternoon in the relative comfort of the dry-floored, elevated blinds.

Major Peabody was disappointed. In response to his request for another drawing of the straws, his three dry companions made disagreeable comments. "Excuse me, Major, but I don't recall any agreement limiting your water time to a single morning," said Rob Cowdery, Peabody's favorite duck-hunting companion.

"That's right. I don't believe it was even limited to a single day," agreed the Major's longtime friend Steve Gress, who then added: "It's only five more days. I'm sure you'll get used to it. You may even get to like it."

The other hunter, Jim Larson, was sympathetic. "We should take pity on him and give him a fair chance," he said. "Let's put it to a vote."

They did. The Major lost—three to one.

Late in the afternoon, Peabody sat on a wooden chair next to a small desk in his room at the Arbol Grande *finca*. He would have been more comfortable sitting on the bed, but he didn't want to soil either the blanket covering it or the throw rug that lay beside it on the tiled floor.

He was still caked with the mud he had acquired from standing in Lago Playita. Dust from the road on the return trip had adhered to whatever part of his clothing retained any of the lake's water and to whatever part of his body that had been moistened by the sweat that poured from him during the hot afternoon exertions.

He finished a bottle of Nicaraguan beer. Refreshed, he felt up to the problem of removing his clothing. He first kicked his boots together to loosen both the larger chunks of dried lake-bottom mud and the lake plants that were cemented to them. The dust covering his hands and fingers left them dry, and they slipped from the laces. He had to get a good grip to loosen the boots.

As he rose to remove his shirt, he saw himself in the mirror above the desk. The powdery dust had entered and accentuated every line on his face. It turned his dark eyebrows, mustache, and hair to gray. "My God," he said to himself. "That's what I'll look like if I ever decide to get old."

The Best of the Major

Major Peabody carried his boots and clothing with him into the shower. As he washed what he considered to be a taxable portion of northwestern Nicaragua real estate from his hide, layers of dirt washed off the clothing that lay beneath his feet.

He wiped his boots, shoved crumpled newspaper inside them, and hoped they would be dry enough to be comfortable for the next day's hunt. Then he dressed and walked to the patio to join his friends, who were already seated around a table and enjoying a post-hunt libation.

"You clean up pretty well for a man who can't hit a duck passing to his right," said Larson as he added some Glenlivet to the ice and water in the glass waiting before the Major's empty chair.

And as he relaxed with his friends, Major Nathaniel Peabody, USA (ret.) thought, "How nice it is to be here rather than in all the mud and dirt of Philadelphia."

22

UPMANN, PARTAGAS, ETC.

Open the old cigar box. Get me a Cuban stout,
For things are running crossways, and Maggie and I are out.
We quarreled about Havanas. We fought o'er a good cheroot.
And I know she is exacting—and she says I am a brute . . .
A million surplus Maggies are willing to bear the yoke;
And a woman is only a woman, but a good cigar is a smoke.

Rudyard Kipling
The Betrothed

MAJOR NATHANIEL PEABODY ENJOYED FINE CIGARS. He claimed a clear and legal right to smoke them—the same kind of right that, he claimed, authorized his almost constant shotgunning activities. When my attorney's training led me to question him concerning the exact source of his supposed "right," he directed me to the preamble of the United States Constitution and, in particular, to the phrase, "Promote the general welfare and secure the blessings of liberty."

Major Peabody's one marriage was a disaster, and I know cigars were among the various irritants that led to the early dissolution of that union. The Major once told me his wife was "quite vocal—constantly—about her belief that cigar smoke polluted the atmosphere."

The amount of time he spent with shotguns and dogs (the four-footed variety) was also, I'm sure, a contributing cause. "With all the good, wealthy women in the world," he once said, "I had to marry one whose interests in upland game birds and retrieving dogs was nearly equal to my own interest in cocktail parties and the ballet."

To be sure I had no opportunity for misinterpretation, he added, "And, as you are well aware, my interest in such matters approaches the non-existent."

I never heard Major Peabody quote Kipling's poem *The Betrothed* directly, but there can be no doubt that he approves of its stated philosophy. Oh, the Major maintains a healthy interest in the opposing sex, and he has engaged in an occasional dalliance, but such healthy interest is not the highest priority in his life. I'd guess the first three are shotgunning, good hunting dogs, and single-malt Scotch whisky. I don't know if quality cigars are fourth or fifth.

The 1969 revolution in Cuba incurred the Major's extreme displeasure. This wasn't a result of strong ideological differences, nor was it a knee-jerk reaction caused by his distaste for the extensive control over and intrusions into the lives of the individual that are basic to all Communist forms of government.

No, Peabody's objections to the regime of Fidel Castro were measured and well reasoned. They were based on the embargoes placed on Cuban cigars and on the serious limitations placed on the Major's opportunities to again hunt ducks and doves in the island republic. Peabody suffered under these burdens for more than three decades. He liked Cuba almost as much as he disliked Castro and often spoke, almost wistfully, of duck hunting in that country's rice fields and of its H. Upmann #6 cigars.

Somehow, it wasn't a surprise when the Major informed me that he and a pair of his cronies had contacted the Cuban tourist bureau in Toronto and had arranged a hunting trip to Cuba via Canada.

It *was* a surprise when he announced that he had made similar arrangements for me. I had no intention of going to Cuba. I don't speak Spanish. I'm not a duck or dove hunter. I'm a lousy shot, even with those guns that scatter hundreds of tiny pellets all over a wide area. I don't smoke cigars. It was probably against the law for a U.S. citizen to go to Cuba. And I didn't want to go.

I immediately voiced those objections. Holding a cigar between his fingers, the Major waved his hand in the air as if he was brushing away unseen crumbs. He didn't argue. He merely stated that he would be in Cuba on the first day of the month. Since it was my legal obligation to deliver his spendthrift-trust check to him at that time, I'd have to be there anyway. And all arrangements had been made.

Cuba, the Major told me, claims to house over fifty million doves. He said it also harbors some millions of what they call *yaguasin*, a bird we are apt to call a fulvous tree duck. The paucity of natural predators on the island and the extensive rice plantings there account for the proliferation of these species. A large number of both kinds of birds are found in Pinar del Rio, the westernmost province of the republic.

Pinar del Rio is also the place where an aromatic fruit called the *guayabito* is grown. That fruit can be made into a brandy, locally referred to as *guayabito seco*. *Guayabito seco* is respected by those who have had the temerity to overimbibe when first introduced to it. Major Peabody could have warned me but didn't.

While *guayabito* seco may have influenced the Major's friends to decide to go to Pinar del Rio's Maspoton Hunting and Fishing Club for their foray, I suspect there was a more important reason. The fact that Pinar del Rio is the province where some of Cuba's finest cigar tobacco is grown was of even more importance in the selection of that site.

As noted elsewhere, the Major inclines toward the use of his well-preserved 20-gauge English stocked, double-barreled Lefever for use on doves. When he demanded I buy two 12-gauge doubles, I was not unmindful of the implied slur on my wingshooting abilities. At the time I thought, I can miss them just as well with a 20-gauge shotgun as I can with a 12-gauge.

But the Major was the expert. I followed his advice and was properly provisioned when we arrived in the province of Pinar del Rio.

Cuban hunting regulations establish the hunter's maximum daily bag limit at one hundred doves. I did no damage to the dove population during our morning hunts. All I got was a very sore shoulder. During the afternoon, we hunted ducks. The limit was forty per day. This limit, too, was highly academic as far as I was concerned.

After the evening meals, when the hunters reported the day's body count over *guayabito seco* and cigars, I tried to save face by proclaiming to be a dedicated catch-and-release man. Major Peabody came to my defense. He said I shot well "on average." I took this to be a compliment until he explained that I shot three feet behind the doves and three feet ahead of the ducks.

Still, I must admit I enjoyed it all. Watching all those doves fly past me in the mornings; frightening fulvous tree ducks in the afternoon while standing on a platform built high in the branches of a mangrove thicket; and listening to the Major and his friends tell outrageous lies (and keep straight faces)—these were all memorable and pleasant experiences.

The evening before we left Havana and boarded the flight back to Toronto, the reason why I had been invited to accompany the other hunters became apparent. Major Peabody came into my room and gave me 100 cigars. A hundred cigars was the maximum number a person could bring through customs without paying an import tax.

Peabody knew that I didn't smoke. He knew I wouldn't keep the cigars for myself. By forcing me to join the hunt, Peabody doubled his own cigar import quota. I had spent $4,250 on shotguns and air transportation for the sole purpose of providing the Major with an extra 100 Cuban cigars.

Actually, the total cost was much higher. When I passed through customs in New York, on the trip back from Toronto, I declared the 100 cigars. The Major was not behind me. He had quietly slipped away and was in another line. The customs official who checked my gear discovered another twenty-four cigars in my baggage.

Two dozen five-inch, H. Upmann #6 cigars with a 42 ring size will fit into and fill the barrels of two 12-gauge double-barreled shotguns. The twenty-four cigars and my new shotguns were confiscated.

23

Thus Spake Major Peabody

MAJOR PEABODY SET THE PITCHER OF WATER, the ice cubes, and the recently opened bottle of single-malt Scotch whisky on the end table next to the humidor. As he settled back in his chair before the fireplace, he said: "Help yourself to a libation and a smoke, young man. As a proper host, it's the least I can offer. After all, you provided my supply of both of them."

It was, indeed, the least he could offer. Though it was February, the shortest month of the year, the liquid assets of Major Nathaniel Peabody amounted to pocket change and nothing more. He had invited me to dinner (I knew the bill would come to me) and then conned me into paying for a replenishment of his supplies of scotch and Honduran cigars.

Now, we were in his Philadelphia apartment, waiting for midnight. Earlier in the month, a number of very good but second-best poker hands had ruined the Major's cash position, and on his return from a South Dakota pheasant hunt, the lack of funds required the Major to stay at home, where he quickly depleted his cache of food, drink, and cigars.

Peabody's spendthrift-trust check was safely resting in an envelope inside my coat jacket. Oh, how I wished I had been authorized to give it to him before the first of the month. If he had been in possession of that check, he would have been able to pay for the evening's expenses. As it was, I knew my own investment would never be returned.

Apparently the loss at the poker table still irked Major Peabody, for he seemed a bit moody at dinner and now was unaccustomedly quiet. And it was still more than an hour before I could deliver his monthly stipend.

As we have established, I am not a shotgunner and dogs don't like me. I am the antithesis of Major Peabody. So it was difficult for me to find a topic of conversation that might bring him out of his brown study. Whenever he was forced to stay in his apartment, the Major passed the time by reading. Among the books and magazines on the floor beside his chair, I saw a copy of Walt Whitman's *Leaves of Grass*.

"Ah," I said, "you're reading *Leaves of Grass*, and, intending to impress him, I quoted, " 'I think that I could turn and live with animals, they are so placid and self-contained.' " This brought the Major to attention.

"Interesting man, Walt Whitman. I'm sure he was a city boy," he said, pausing and looking directly at me. Then, still looking directly at me, he added, "At least he wasn't very knowledgeable about the animal world." I got his point. Then the Major sank back into the chair and began his soliloquy.

"Whitman was a hospital attendant during the War Between the States. Later he got a government job working in the patent office in Washington, D.C. That experience must have unnerved him. Apparently he took leave of his senses, became a poet, and wrote the lines you quote.

"After someone lives in Washington, D.C., for a few years, it's understandable why he might prefer to live with animals. Even today, a reasonable man would rather share his cabin with a weasel than with any run-of-the-mill member of the House of Representatives.

"But that doesn't mean reasonable men want to take up house-keeping with weasels—or any animal, for that matter. Establishing residence in a pigsty or sharing barn space with a cow is, obviously, a pretty messy operation. The same objection can be registered with regard to living with other domestic animals like horses, goats, llamas, sheep, et cetera. (The Major later pointed out that competent zoologists do not classify hunting dogs as animals. Living with hunting dogs is perfectly all right.)

"This leaves wild animals. Though Whitman may have been emotionally—and, some think, intellectually—compatible with squirrels, living with them is out of the question. A good number of people are afraid of high places, and squirrel nests are notoriously cold in the wintertime. While Walt might have considered living in a tree with a squirrel, just how would a squirrel have reacted to living with Walt? Wild animals, in general are highly territorial.

"Anyone who tries to share space with an animal is in for a lot of trouble. A raccoon, for example, can be expected to get testy if you crawl into its hollow log. And if you think a raccoon can be hostile, try moving in with a mink or a bobcat or a badger.

"Then there are the animal-rights people. They can be counted on to start a lawsuit claiming harassment of their four-legged friends. Moreover, I'm sure any competent judge will call for a hearing before the sanity commission if he gets wind of a citizen crawling up a tree to live with the squirrels.

"I can understand why Whitman voiced his rejection of association with humans. A few years in Washington can make a man say silly things. We hear them from senators every day. However, not satisfied with merely stating an insane preference for cohabitation with beasts, Whitman felt it necessary to expand his thesis and go on to claim animals are 'placid and self-contained.'

"That canard is beyond the pale. Perhaps, as Whitman claims, some animals are placid and self-contained. The three-toed sloth and the brood sow come to mind. However, Walt didn't say, 'I think I could turn and live with brood sows and three-toed sloths, they are so placid and self-contained.' No. He assigned a placid nature to the entire animal world.

"The animal world is neither placid nor self-contained. It is red of fang and claw. All credible evidence proves it. Television's Gentle Ben to the contrary, bear are not placid. Come up on one while you are searching a raspberry patch for ruffed grouse, and you'll hear a growl that could frighten the living bejeezus out of Ivan the Terrible. A great deal of violence will occur if you don't quickly put a lot of distance between you and the animal.

"It was not Dorothy in *The Wizard of Oz* who coined the phrase 'Lions and tigers and bears, oh my.' " It was the early Christians. Contact the spirit of any Christian who spent a Sunday afternoon as part of the entertainment in the Roman Coliseum. He will assure you that animals are not at all placid.

"And as far as the 'self-contained' is concerned, need I point out that when the lions and tigers and bears left the Roman Coliseum arena, it was not the 'self' they 'contained'? It was the Christians.

"Today the Coliseum is out of business, and the practice of

feeding Christians to nonplacid, sharp-toothed animals has been eliminated as a public celebration in many parts of the world. Sunday afternoons are dedicated to another spectator sport—football, a violent game composed of teams named after violent animals—Lions and Bengals and Bears, oh my.

"If anyone persists in believing that Walt Whitman knew what he was taking about when he characterized animals as 'placid,' he might engage a wolverine in friendly conversation. If he recovers and is still of the same belief, as soon as the stitches are removed, he might try to pet a porcupine.

"Whitman's suggestion of turning and living with animals is completely ridiculous. If he'd had his wits about him, he would have left Washington, moved to some uncivilized place like Brooklyn, become a journalist, and forgotten all that nonsense about wanting to live with animals."

The Major had recovered and was his old self again.

24

UNCLE CALHOUN—PART II

MAJOR PEABODY WAS TELLING ME ABOUT HIS Uncle Calhoun's favorite shotgun. He described it as a 1925-vintage Lefever double barrel. It was choked cylinder and improved-cylinder, had an English stock, and sported twenty-four-inch barrels. I noticed that Major Peabody owned the same kind of weapon and presumed it had once belonged to Calhoun Peabody. The Major confirmed my suspicion and told me how it came into his possession.

The conversation took place during the evening of the last day of the month. We were again in my apartment as we awaited the stroke of midnight, when I was authorized to deliver Peabody's spendthrift-trust remittance.

"Uncle Calhoun Peabody never set foot in a commercial airplane," said the Major as he lit one of the H. Upmann cigars he had ordered his tobacconist to send me (along with the bill). He rattled the ice in his empty glass. It was his signal that I should take it to the kitchen and renew it with more cubes and single-malt Scotch whisky.

"It may have been a fear of high places, but I doubt it," he went on. "You see, he never traveled without his dog or his shotgun. The first time he tried to use air transportation, a narrow-minded air-line employee stopped him at the gate and told him he couldn't take his English pointer aboard with him.

"Uncle Calhoun thought the man was joking and pressed on. But the man was serious and claimed it was against company pol-icy to allow dogs into the passengers' compartment. You may not believe it, but that same idiotic policy remains in effect to this very day.

"Uncle Calhoun contended that the dog was better trained and better behaved than most of the other passengers. Two host-esses, without even knowing the dog, agreed. But the pointer was not allowed on the plane. From that moment on, Uncle Calhoun used surface transportation only. He never set foot in an airliner.

"In addition to despising the airlines, Uncle Calhoun carried a deep and abiding grudge against insurance companies. Though he enjoyed the commissions they paid him for selling the farms they owned via mortgage foreclosure, he never really forgave them for posting good quail country with 'No Trespassing' signs.

"Sooner or later, age may catch up with us all. [The Major said 'may' because he never expected to get old. And it's possible he was right.] It caught up with Uncle Calhoun," he continued. "His legs gave out, and he could no longer spend his days walking the fields in search of quail.

"So, together with his dog and his 20-gauge Lefever, Calhoun boarded a train and went to Atlanta, where he took an apartment in a building owned by another quail hunter who had no objection to either hunting dogs or tenants who spent hours cleaning shot-guns.

"A few years later, the president of an Atlanta insurance company contacted Great Aunt Aurora. He complained that Calhoun Peabody would periodically appear in the home office of the company in downtown Atlanta. Accompanied by a dog, my uncle would loudly proclaim that he owned the property. He would try to nail 'No Trespassing' signs on the walls, menace the employees with his cane, and demand that everyone get off his property under pain of an action for criminal trespass.

"The insurance-company president told Great Aunt Aurora that Calhoun Peabody should be put away.

"Well, black sheep or no black sheep, Great Aunt Aurora would never allow her nephew to be 'put away.' She was aware of our close friendship and asked me to talk him into moving to Charlottesville, where he could live in the family homestead.

"Uncle Calhoun immediately recognized me when I went to visit him in Atlanta, but it quickly became apparent that arteriosclerosis was having its effect. From time to time, he left reality behind and retreated to a place existing only in his memory and imagination." The Major paused, relit his cigar, and thought for a moment. "You know, young man," he said to me, "given the kind of lifestyle imposed upon us by today's society, leaving reality behind isn't necessarily a bad idea." Then he continued his story.

"I told Uncle Calhoun we were going to take a train ride to Virginia, where we would hunt one of the old family farms. I told him about hearing the peeping calls of large coveys of quail. A sparkle came to his eye, and he agreed to the trip.

"Uncle Calhoun wasn't against partaking of Tennessee charcoal-filtered corn whiskey. In his youth, he was able to carry quite a bit of it without wobbling to the right or left. During the last twenty years, however, his capacity had dramatically declined. With ten ounces of the stuff inside him, he was easily convinced that the airport was the depot and the plane was a train.

"He was in jovial spirits when we deplaned at the Charlottesville airport. He whispered in the ear of the hostess, who blushed quaintly but, nevertheless, smiled at him. I collected his shotgun and baggage and turned him over to Great Aunt Aurora. When his dog, an old English pointer named George III, arrived a few days later by train, their reunion was touching, and Uncle Calhoun soon became accustomed to his new surroundings.

"It bothered me to have used the potential of a quail hunt as a ruse to get Uncle Calhoun back to the family homestead." The Major again paused and looked at me. "That's the only time my conscience has bothered me—probably because I am so otherwise pure of thought and deed." Major Peabody kept a straight face when he made that comment. I think he actually believed it.

"A year later, I determined to set the matter straight. I went to Charlottesville to make good on my word. George III was a very old dog then. He was gray and gouty, weak of eye, and rheumatic. Uncle Calhoun was pretty much in the same condition. I took them both to a hunt club. We were all driven to a likely spot where the ground was level and the cover light.

"I followed Uncle Calhoun as he hobbled after George, who— with equally unsteady gait—held his nose to the ground and wagged his tail, remembering his days in the field. It took only a few minutes before George stiffened, tentatively lifted his paw, and told us quail were there.

"Uncle Calhoun advanced to the dog. He fired once as the quail exploded from the cover. George moved forward and picked up a bird. As he turned to bring it back, Uncle Calhoun put the butt of his Lefever on the ground and let the gun drop.

"Then he walked toward George and got down on his knees. George dropped the bird on the ground before him. The old man put his arms around the dog and wept.

"Within six months, they were both dead. I believe the dog died first. Great Aunt Aurora gave me the Lefever."

Major Peabody rose from the chair and left my apartment without a word. It was after midnight. He hadn't asked for his check.

25

THE PRIMORDIAL INSTINCT

WHEN MAJOR NATHANIEL PEABODY RATTLED the ice cubes in his empty glass for the second time, I refilled it and returned it to him.

"Amazing," he said. "It must be extrasensory perception—your knowing I was ready for another drink."

"Oh," I answered, "it may be merely a matter of instinct."

"No," said the Major, "I don't think so. Instinct is something quite different. Birds and animals, even insects, have these ancient urges, these primordial instincts. Human beings seem to have lost them. At best, we retain only vague memories of them. Let me give you an example.

"The Arctic tern annually leaves the northernmost parts of Canada and flies south, across the equator and on through Argentina to the Antarctic. A few months later, it flies back again. The distance of its astounding flight is some forty-five thousand miles. And the bird accomplishes this feat without the benefit of a compass, a sextant, a map, or any assistance from a global positioning satellite.

"Now let's compare the tern's ability with that of the human being. The man we elected and sent to Washington last year still can't find his way to the Senate bathroom.

"The Arctic tern and the senator do, however, share at least one characteristic. In these latitudes, both are seen only during the migratory season—the tern in the fall while on its way to the Antarctic, and the senator during the months immediately preceding an election, when he flies to his constituents for hand shaking, fund-raising, and ritualistic lying.

"However, a few of the human kind, and I include myself within the group, have retained substantially more than mere vestiges of the primordial instincts. My own internal clock gives me a strong migratory urge every September. Maybe it's the reducing number of minutes of daylight or the drop in temperature or the changes in tidal pull, but, like the wild goose, I feel that irresistible urge to make an annual autumnal trek."

Translated into English, this meant the Major was about to make his yearly visit to northern Ontario. Yes, his trips to Henry Hudson's Bay coincided with the migration of the geese, but as they flew south, the Major flew north. He would meet them at the mouth of the Winisk River, halfway between Lake River and Fort Severen, on the southern shore of the bay.

This trip was certainly on his mind as he sank deeper into the chair and, almost mesmerized, began to talk about last year's hunt.

"Doc Carmichael and I always have a good time at the Winisk. I like to hunt with him. Last year we got as far as Timmons and had to spend the night there. We'd met a wingshooter named Jerry Koenig, who was also on his way to the Winisk River, so we all joined forces and went out in search of a steak.

"Someday I'll write a book identifying restaurants that hunters should avoid. The steak we got in Timmons was so tough it made my teeth hurt. Moreover, there was no establishment where we could purchase liquids to soothe the terrible pain of toothache.

"When we became aware of that atrocity, Jerry invited us into his room, where we sampled some of the supply of homemade wine he had brought with him. It had a dry, sherrylike taste and was delicious. I had the suspicion I was going to like this man.

"The next morning we finished the final leg of the journey, landing at an abandoned World War II Canadian Air Force base near Hudson's Bay. The Doc and I bunked in together at a goose camp operated by the Chippewa Indians. Jerry was assigned a single room.

"Each morning, the three of us and a guide would leave the camp before sunrise. We'd find a suitable location and build a willow-switch blind. The goose decoys would be set before there was enough light to distinguish the forms of the birds that were noisily rocketing over our heads.

"At three or four in the afternoon, we'd be back in camp for a wash-up. Dinner was followed by a bit of socializing, but not too much because wake-up time was disgustingly early. Jerry would invite me to his room for a glass of wine. He never included Doc Carmichael in the invitation.

"You get to know a man if you hunt with him for a week. I enjoyed Jerry Koenig's company. He carried his weight, told good stories, and shot well—but not so well that we had reason to become jealous of him. Our friendship was sealed when I learned he, too, maintained a deep-seated grudge against convicted felons, drug pushers, and saxophone players.

"On our last day in camp, the geese were flying. We decided to reduce the weight of our luggage by shooting our remaining ammunition. I used all of my shells, and Jerry gave his last three to Doc Carmichael so he could fire the final salvo of the hunt. I thought it was a great gesture, and it confirmed my opinion of Jerry.

"We spent an evening together in Toronto, then Doc Carmichael and I returned to Philadelphia, and Jerry caught a flight to Milwaukee. I liked Jerry and hoped we'd hunt together again. I suggested the Doc and I invite him to join us during a South Dakota pheasant expedition. But Doc Carmichael had reservations.

"I couldn't understand it. Jerry had given Doc his last three shotgun shells on the Winisk goose hunt. Certainly that was a friendly thing to do. The explanation, however, was forthcoming. It was because Jerry never invited the Doc into his Winisk quarters.

"I feel partly responsible for the Doc's unfortunate attitude. I suppose I shouldn't have told Jerry that Doc Carmichael was an alcoholic, that his wife had pleaded with me to keep him sober, and that the fermented grape was absolutely lethal to Doc's constitution.

"If I ever see Jerry again, I'll confess that what I told him was not entirely accurate. He should be told, I suppose, that Doc Carmichael is neither an alcoholic nor a married man.

"I don't believe I can be blamed for my actions at the Winisk goose camp. What I did was, really, a kind of automatic reflex. It amounted to an example of a sensitive human being's exercise of that primordial, instinctive urge for self-preservation.

"By keeping Doc Carmichael out of the room, I was preserving Jerry's wine for myself."

26

CONVERSATION IN A DUCK BLIND

IT WAS THE SECOND DAY OF NOVEMBER, and I was in a duck blind in Canada with Major Nathaniel Peabody. I had delivered his monthly spendthrift-trust and retirement checks but, due to rain and overcast, was unable to convince the bush pilot to take me back to civilization.

He told me he was a middle-aged bush pilot. He told me most of the bush pilots were young. He told me he attained middle age because he refused to fly in weather "like this." Then he turned his back and opened another can of Moosehead beer.

Of course, the Major was pleased with the inclement conditions. It was great weather for ducks. That morning it was cold, and so was I. For a time, the ducks flew over the decoys, and the Major shot at them. Then he either smiled or swore, and the dog swam out and brought them back or remained in the blind and gave the Major a reproachful look.

An hour after sunrise, the wind stopped blowing and the rain stopped falling and the ducks stopped flying. Being, therefore, less miserable, I stopped thinking of how uncomfortable I was and began to think of how much I would rather have been in Philadelphia. And then it occurred to me.

"Major," I said, getting his attention, "do you know that today is election day, and this will be the first time I have not voted since attaining age eighteen?"

"I understand election day occurs sometime in November," he answered as he vainly searched the sky for flying ducks and scratched the dog's ears. "I can recall voting for Harry Truman—and, later, I believe, for Dwight Eisenhower. I suppose I voted for House and Senate office seekers at the same time. I have no specific recollection."

"And you haven't voted since then?" I blurted in disbelief. "Aren't you upset with what those scoundrels in Congress do? Sex, dope, bribery, the widespread assumption they are above the law—doesn't any of that bother you enough to vote them out of office?"

"No," answered the Major. "I'm quite satisfied with the senators and representatives in Washington. Presumably, the rest of the voting public shares my satisfaction. They consistently reelect and reelect and reelect their representative—in spite of his history of scandalous, autocratic, unprincipled, and self-serving actions."

"But," I argued, "with your obvious recognition of the unethical and fraudulent activities that run rampant in government, wouldn't it be refreshing to elect someone with higher principals?"

"Oh, I'm sure that at this very moment, in duck blinds, in grouse coverts, and in quail and pheasant fields there are enough hunters who could case their weapons, go into town, vote, and throw the rascals out—thereby upgrading both the IQ and the ethical coefficient of Congress.

"But, my young friend," he continued, "hunters tend to be

intelligent folk and do not want that result." The Major did not smile, nor was there a twinkle in his eye as he delivered that astounding statement. He was dead serious. I couldn't believe my own ears!

Peabody looked at me and said: "Your expression suggests you can't believe your own ears. I'm amazed by your reaction. In this grand republic, you know, there are a multitude of moronic situations existing in and out of the political arena. If you were a visitor from some strange place and with no understanding of how our democracy works—say from Mars or Europe or Massachusetts—it might appear as if the public were unaware or uninterested in such situations. And you would be wrong.

"For instance, take the penal system. If some felon is charged with a serious crime involving a gun, the jury does its duty and the judge sentences him to twenty years at soft labor. Then what happens? The parole board lets him out in three years.

"Then there's the matter of so-called prison overcrowding. It may soon be common to hear a judge say: 'You have been convicted of murder in the first degree, and I sentence you to life imprisonment. However, since all available prison cells are currently occupied, your name will be put on a waiting list, and whenever a cell becomes available, you will be sent to prison. In the meantime please keep the probation and parole people advised of your whereabouts.'

"It is my contention that the people have already addressed both the election and the prison problems." The Major paused and again scanned the sky for incoming ducks. He seemed willing to let the conversation drop at that point.

I waited a full minute for an explanation of his last statement, but none was forthcoming. I therefore asked, "How so?"

"It's obvious," he answered. "We've already established the fact that hunters don't vote because they are pleased with the results produced by both presidential and congressional elections. And we both know hunters are admirable folk with intelligence quotients substantially above the average.

"In the rest of the population, there are others like you who, with a certain amount of both logic and evidence, believe Congress is composed of scoundrels who should be thrown out of office—or perhaps have their terms limited to a fixed number of years in office.

"A maximum term of eight years has been proposed. I'd guess eight years has been selected because it is felt a politician should be able to steal enough during that period to last his entire lifetime. And if he can't steal that much in eight years, he is too incompetent to continue in office. These are cogent and defensible positions, but I'm afraid they miss the whole point of the matter.

"You see, when society is confronted by a malefactor, drunk, felon, or pervert, he can be charged with a crime, found guilty, and sentenced to twenty years in prison. But, as I have said, he will be paroled and back in town in three years, again bedeviling the honest folk of his community.

"If, on the other hand, such an individual is elected into the Senate, he will be gone for at least a full six years. He'll get no automatic appeal. There will be no possibility of this elected felon's receiving a parole.

"For lesser crimes, suspected malfeasors can be elected to the presidency for four years or to the House of Representatives for two. And if they don't mend their ways, they can be reelected for additional terms. The electorate can keep sending them to Washington, D.C., thereby keeping them away from respectable people.

"The mere fact that most of our congressmen and congresswomen, as well as their friends with the patronage jobs, are corrupt shouldn't shock you. It doesn't shock me. They're politicians. It's the nature of the beast. You might just as well be shocked by the fact that dogs bark."

After a moment's pause, the Major looked at me and said: "I am shocked by your implied suggestion that we defeat them at the polls, thereby running the risk they will return to their hometowns where, I'm sure, many honest and defenseless citizens reside."

As I thought about the matter and began to nod my head in agreement, three mallard flew over the blocks. The Major dropped one of them. The dog was happy.

27

BAD LUCK

AFTER DINNER, MAJOR PEABODY SELECTED an H. Upmann cigar from the box proffered by the waiter. He declined the use of the restaurant's clipper and used the one he carried in the breast pocket of his sport coat. He leaned back in the chair and expelled a cloud of smoke, seeming a trifle sullen.

When the Major returns from one of his early-fall goose hunts in northern Manitoba, he can be expected to be tired but in excellent spirits. That three-day hunt is an autumnal ritual for him, Doc Carmichael, an attorney from Fort Wayne, and an engineer from Seattle. But when I picked him up at the airport this time, the Major was not his usual garrulous self. He looked unhappy.

I noticed that the first and second fingers of his right hand were taped together. He had offered no explanation and I didn't ask for one. Major Peabody maintained his silent and morose mood for the duration of the drive back to his apartment, so I invited him to dine with me at Bookbinders. I was sure that a good meal (paid for by someone else) would elevate his spirits.

The Major, however, was not that easily consoled. He gazed up at the ceiling of the restaurant, looking at nothing in particular and, obviously, contemplating something distasteful. Finally he said: "We live in a time of great moral decay. Believe me, my boy, you simply can't trust anyone any more." And then he was silent.

I waited a few moments and decided to end his brown study. "How was the hunt, Major?" I inquired, as brightly as I could. He glared at me and said nothing. I tried again. "What happened to your fingers?"

Major Peabody set his cigar on the ashtray and said, "I suppose your infinite curiosity won't be satisfied until you've received a full report." Then he told me about the hunt.

"The Beaver was fitted out with floats, and we landed at the outfitter's seaplane base at the south end of the lake. Two guides were waiting with two boats, one old and one new. After piling our shotguns and baggage into the beat-up boat with the dented motor, the four of us got into the new rig and we all headed north. First we ran to the head of the lake and, then, up a meandering river that led to the open areas we planned to hunt.

"It was a gray, cloudy day with, at first, only moderate wind and rain. I kept my eye on the boat carrying our gear and watched as we slowly outdistanced it. Before long, the mist came on and I could hardly see the other guide, now far behind us. Shortly thereafter, the temperature dropped precipitously, the wind began to rise, and the rain got heavier. I wondered what would happen if the boat swamped."

A terrifying scene came to mind, and I said, "Good heavens, Major, in that cold water, none of you could survive for long. Hypothermia would—"

"No, no, no, you don't understand," Major Peabody interrupted. "I was worried about the boat carrying our gear. If it tipped over, we'd lose our shotguns. I can tell you I experienced an ominous premonition that I wouldn't fire a gun during the entire hunt.

"The weather was miserable when we finally got to the outfitter's cabin. I stood on the dock in the wind and the rain, anxiously waiting for the second boat. I had visions of my Lefever double barrel rusting away on the bottom of the river. But the second guide eventually brought the boat to the dock, and I was relieved to see him pull my leg-o'-mutton gun case from beneath a tarpaulin. Unfortunately, in my hurry to retrieve it and get inside the cabin, out of the rain, I didn't exercise my usual caution.

"I slipped on the dock, performed an aerial maneuver that would do credit to a gold medal Olympic gymnast, and landed with my full weight on the exact tip of my trigger finger." Peabody stopped and looked at me. "I said 'Ouch,' " he continued, "and, I believe, a few other things."

"Oh," I said, "What bad luck."

"Bad luck, indeed," answered the Major. "And if you think this tragedy elicited other than guffaws from those three scoundrels in my hunting party, you are wrong, wrong, wrong."

The Major raised his right hand, looked at the taped first and second fingers of his right hand, and—using his thumb and his third and fourth fingers—picked up his scotch and water, emptied it, and motioned the waiter for a refill.

"Doc Carmichael gave my forefinger a vicious jerk in order to pull it back where it belonged—and, I am sure, for the additional purpose of torturing me. Then he taped it to my middle finger in order to keep it immobile—and, I am equally sure, for the additional purpose of making certain I couldn't shoot my shotgun."

"Bad luck, Major," I said.

"Bad luck, indeed," he answered. "Especially since we had our usual agreement—every day, the most successful hunter would get a hundred-dollar contribution from each of the others. Being *hors de combat* and pointing to my painful, overbandaged trigger finger, I appealed to their senses of decency and honor and asked to be excused from participating in the contest.

"Well," he continued, "my plea was the cause of great hilarity and mirth, punctuated at regular intervals with comments like: 'No Way, José,' and 'Payback time.' I started that hunt with the reasonable expectation of collecting a minimum of five hundred dollars from the shoot; I ended up paying out three hundred."

"Bad luck, Major," I again said.

"Bad luck, indeed," he again answered. "Still," he continued, "it has always been my conviction that adversity represents only a challenge that can be overcome by the stalwart man. I paid fifty dollars to the guide who ran the good boat and made a suggestion to him. In return, he assured me that when we returned to the seaplane base at the end of the hunt, the slow boat carrying our weapons and baggage would, at the last moment, surge ahead of the one he operated and beat us to the outfitter's dock.

"The pain seemed to subside from my broken finger, and I was able to withstand the disrespectful and rude commentaries made by my three companions for the duration of the hunt. I knew justice would triumph in the end.

"The guide returned my wink when we got into his motor boat and started the trip back down river. Each of my three hunting associates (I no longer called them friends) accepted my hundred-dollar wager that the baggage boat would get to the seaplane before we did. The recovery of that three hundred dollars would put me close to even and avoid impending financial disaster."

Major Peabody paused. He sipped from the glass in his injured hand. He scowled. Through clenched teeth he said: "That deceptive, rascally guide who winked at me in confirmation of our agreement had already informed Doc Carmichael of our pact. Then he took seventy-five dollars from the doctor and agreed to do something dishonorable—he wouldn't throw the race; he'd win it.

"I tell you, the only honest people left in this world are the professional wrestlers. Their word is good. When they are paid to throw a fight, you can count on them. They'll throw the fight."

In view of the Major's desolation and pathetic financial situation, I loaned him six hundred dollars. His dejection immediately disappeared, and he was again his buoyant and cheerful self.

A month later I met Dr. Carmichael in the Philadelphia Club. I chastised him and his friends for insisting the Major stick to a goose-hunting bet when he had a broken finger.

Doctor Carmichael didn't know what I was talking about. He told me Peabody had never injured a finger, and, in fact, had won nine hundred dollars from his cronies during the Canada goose hunt. He told me the Major got another three hundred from them when he bet that the old scow carrying their hunting equipment would reach the seaplane base before they did. Doc also told me how the Major had said he needed only another five hundred dollars to afford a pricey trek to Argentina to hunt Magellan and ashy head geese. He further said the Major had formulated a plan to get the money but wouldn't tell them about it.

Doc Carmichael saw the look on my face and began to laugh. "He didn't get it from you, did he?" I nodded, slowly. "I'm afraid you've seen the last of that investment," and he added, "Bad luck."

Bad luck, indeed, I thought.

28

A Bear in Camp

"THE ANIMAL-RIGHTS PEOPLE, IT SEEMS TO ME, are selling a flawed product," said Major Peabody. "Their position appears to be founded in anthropomorphism—the assignment of the characteristics and emotions of human beings to insects, fish, birds, and animals. Ergo, they say, animals are entitled to human-associated rights.

"Of course, there is some limited evidence to show that lower forms of life and humans share some traits. For instance, the black widow spider kills and eats her husband after mating. In the case of the human female, this also occurs, but, usually, it is done symbolically. More than one husband has asked, 'Where is the life that once I led?'

"But in spite of such occasional parallels, I object to the animal-rights folks' broad-brush treatment of the concept.

"The *homo sapiens*, I am told, is programmed to adopt monogamy and what are commonly called 'family values.' By contrast, immediately after procreation, male deer abandon their mates and leave them to fend for themselves. And I've never heard anyone favorably compare the family life of the Komodo dragon with that of the human being.

"No, animals should not be treated as human. They are different. Only in fairy tales will Papa Bear take an offspring out for a walk while the porridge cools and Goldilocks undertakes her felonious breaking, entering, and stealing. Papa bear will kill his own young and eat them if he gets the chance."

The Major spent a moment or two in contemplation and added, "After a review of the present-day activities of human youth, the practice of infanticide, adopted throughout the bear community, has much to recommend it."

The Major looked at me, meaningfully rattled the ice cubes in his empty glass, and continued: "I know making such comments is politically incorrect and might be considered an example of outrageous discrimination. Still, I will stand by them. And I will happily go farther down that slippery slope. I believe it is a slander to the animal kingdom to accuse them of having the characteristics of human beings.

"I hasten to remind you that sloth, greed, alcohol and drug addiction, political corruption, and other such common human qualities are not found in animals. To accuse animals of harboring such traits improperly holds them up to public ridicule and contempt.

"That being said, nevertheless, animals seldom develop the highly perfected capacity for learning that is associated with the *homo sapiens*. Granted, my own personal knowledge and interest in such studies as integral calculus or rocket science are about the same as that of a pine squirrel. But others of my genus, I'm told, have mastered both subjects. I've never met a pine squirrel that could count to eleven.

"In the animal kingdom, most actions are based on instinct.

Over the centuries, we humans have slowly discarded most of our primal instincts and replaced them with an ability to reason. Many people have learned, for instance, that it is particularly dangerous to get between a bear and her cub.

"And therein lies a story," said the Major, as he again rattled the ice in his empty highball glass and caused me to reluctantly open a new bottle of his favorite single-malt Scotch whisky.

"We planned to look for and find woodcock in northern Manitoba. Our guides met us at the fly-in base camp, transferred our gear to motorboats, and took us down the river to the cabin four of us would occupy during the week of our hunt.

"After we had claimed our bunks and hauled our personal gear into the cabin, I broke out my Lefever 20-gauge and began an investigatory stroll around the woods adjoining the campsite. A commotion occurred on my right. I moved toward it and saw a bear cub climbing a fir tree. A mama bear below the tree carefully watched me as I carefully watched her and quickly backed up.

"Personally, I tend to give a wide berth to lady bear and their young offspring. Early in my career, I managed to get between such a pair as I plowed through a deep-woods raspberry patch in search of ruffed grouse. That was when I learned not to shoot a bear with a 20-gauge filled with bird shot. It makes them angry, and one must be quick if one wishes to outrun them.

"That evening, after a dinner of Spam deep fried in Mazola oil, Ellis, our Cree guide, made a classic comment. 'You know,' he said, 'I don't trust that bear.' His suspicion was well founded. During the night, the animal stole a loaf of bread and trashed the camp's open-air kitchen, which was located in an area bordered by the cabin, the guides' tents, and the outhouse.

"The next morning, while breakfasting on eggs and Spam, deep fried in Mazola oil, I suggested that we store the balance of the food in the guides' tent. They suggested it be stored inside our cabin. A compromise was reached, and the foodstuffs were put in a bag and hung from a branch high up in a tree. But we overlooked the flour.

"When we returned to camp that evening, the bear had found it and run off with it. She left a white trail clearly marked on the ground. No one elected to follow it. Instead, we enjoyed a dinner of pork chops, deep fried in Mazola oil.

"Later that night, we awoke to a terrible yelling, swearing, and banging of pots and pans. The ruckus was created by the guides and was occasioned by the bear's attempt to enter their tent. The animal took flight, thereby offering further proof that it had no human qualities. If it had, it might have considered the racket to be an example of modern rock music and applauded, rather than running from it.

"For the balance of the hunt, bear sightings around camp were common during the early-morning and late-evening hours. A symbiotic relationship developed. The bear liked the Mazola oil. Ellis left the pans and tin plates outside. The bear would come and lick them clean. Then Ellis didn't have to wash them.

"Still, we all remembered that it is particularly dangerous to get between an adult bear and her cub. Peace between the human and animal kingdoms reigned until the last morning of the hunt. I awoke early, a man with a mission. I quickly slipped on boots and wool pants, opened the back door of the cabin, and stepped outside.

"Though the sun had not yet risen, there was enough light to see the five-hundred-pound black bear rise up on her back feet, directly in front of me. She was facing me. She looked as if she was only eight feet away, but perhaps it was as much as eight-and-a-half. I didn't need any light to hear her growl.

"I threw the flashlight at her and roared back. I yelled at her to get out of the way and take her kid with her. I must have frightened the hell out of her because that is exactly what she did, post haste.

"And this, my young friend," concluded Major Peabody," is evidence in support of the original thesis that animals don't think like human beings. It is common knowledge that a hunter should never get between a bear and her cub. But those two bear, apparently, had never learned just how dangerous it is for them to get between an outhouse and a hunter who, for a full week, has been subjected to a diet exceedingly rich in Mazola oil.

29

BRANT

"YES?" I SAID INTO MY OFFICE intercom, responding to its buzz.

"That Major person wants to talk to you. Shall I tell him you're busy?" was my secretary's answer. She doesn't like Major Peabody. I suppose he long ago incurred her displeasure by making some politically incorrect comment.

"No, Charlotte," I said. "Please put him through."

The Major went directly to the point. "Do you know any lawyers who live on Fidalgo Island? That's in Puget Sound. In Washington. The state, not D.C." I couldn't imagine what sort of trouble he had gotten into. "What kind of lawyer?" I asked, hoping he wouldn't say "criminal."

"Any kind," he said.

The Smythe, Hauser, Engels & Tauchen law library contains legal directories. I opened my desk copy and went to the Washington section. I read him the appropriate area list of names and telephone numbers, giving him time to write them down.

Then I commented on the consistently high quality and good character of the attorneys who qualified for inclusion in the directory. The Major snorted and said, "You must be insane." Then he hung up. Whenever I talk with Major Peabody, I take every available opportunity to make mention of the consistently high quality and good character of attorneys. I do this because it rankles and bothers and upsets him. It's my way of getting a small measure of revenge for the comments he makes about my profession.

*   *   *

A few days later, Major Peabody flew from Philadelphia to Seattle. He rented a car and drove to the city of Anacortes on the north shore of Fidalgo Island. He immediately began telephoning attorneys. Without preamble or even introducing himself, he asked each one: "What kind of shotgun do you use?"

When he worked his way down to the letter O, he finally received the answer he wanted. A lawyer named Doug Owen admitted to both owning and operating a 16-gauge Lefever. The two men went to lunch, and Peabody explained the purpose of his visit to Anacortes.

Occasionally, an American brant had appeared over the Major's decoys in Maryland, but he had never designed a hunt especially for them. He had no experience with the bird's West Coast cousin, the black brant. Unfortunately, Major Peabody had no close hunting friends in the entire Juan De Fuca archipelago. This was a place where he did not enjoy the benefit of an acquaintance who could show him where the black brant congregate or a friend who could instruct him about local hunting systems and techniques.

Acknowledging his lack of experience in the ways of the black brant, the Major asked for help. Doug Owen took Peabody under his wing and initiated him into the mysteries of Juan De Fuca archipelago hunting. The black brant is a West Coast species. The birds nest along the Bering Strait and the Beaufort Sea in northern

Alaska and Canada. They fly south along the Pacific coast for the winter—as far south as Baja California. The brant arrive in Washington in late September or early October, and the hunting season opens in December.

The bird weighs four to five pounds and is not known to possess an inordinately high IQ. It is a slow flyer, plugging along at forty to forty-five miles an hour. It is easier to call than the snow goose or Canada goose, and it will sometimes incautiously come to a blind in response to nothing more than movement therein.

Brant seldom fly in Vs. They prefer to travel in lines and, while in feeding modes, break up into groups of four to ten birds. They are hunted from blinds built on good-sized rectangular rafts. Silhouette decoys are placed on the corners of the float, and regular decoys fill the spaces between them.

As in the case of all waterfowl, there are times when brant don't fly. These are the interludes when hunters have time to talk and get to know each other. It quickly became apparent to the Major that he had found a kindred spirit. The first indication came when Owen observed that any politician would propose elevating Adolf Hitler to sainthood if he thought it would produce a net gain of a single vote in his favor.

Between shots, the status of crime and punishment in our great republic was analyzed. Peabody was impressed by the Washington attorney's arguments. Owen described the criminal-justice system currently in effect. The philosophy in ascendancy, he said, is that of the sociologists and psychologists, to wit: Whenever someone slaughters his parents, chops up his wife, or robs you at gunpoint, the victim of the crime is, in fact, the perpetrator.

If, through some terrible mistake, he is brought to trial and a jury actually finds him guilty and sends him to prison, the least society can do to correct the error is to put him in a private cell, feed him steak, give him a color television set, fix his teeth, and provide him with complete medical care. Then, in a few months, the parole board will put him back on the street where he can again prove society's guilt by selling dope, assaulting, robbing, and killing.

The parole board, said Owen, is to be applauded, not criticized for its early releases. The cost of maintaining a criminal in prison is horrendous—more expensive that a stay in a posh hotel in Acapulco or Montego Bay. By turning the crook loose at the earliest possible moment, the board is reducing prison costs and saving the taxpayers' money.

As efficient and intelligent as is the present system of crime and punishment, there is still work to be done, pronounced the attorney. The system is flawed. It should be refined, advanced, and improved. The next step to eliminate the flaws in the criminal-justice system will be to educate jurors. They should be required to attend lectures before serving on jury panels. They should be informed of the costs of incarceration, the fact that prison does not rehabilitate, and the probability that the appellate court will overturn any finding of guilt anyway.

Until such time as we begin to put the concept of punishment back into the criminal-justice system, said Owen, jurors might just as well support the social academics, the parole boards, and the liberal judges by finding the criminal not guilty and letting him go, even before he has a chance to get to the prison's revolving doors.

Major Peabody fully enjoyed his expedition to Fidalgo Island

and the hunt for the black brant. When he told me of his various pleasant experiences with the Anacortes lawyer, I repeated my observation of the consistently high quality and good character of attorneys. Peabody corrected me.

He said it was the owners of Lefever shotguns who were of consistently high quality and good character.

CURIOSITY AND THE CATS

MAJOR NATHANIEL PEABODY, USA (RET.) and three Wisconsin friends planned to engage in a late-October grouse hunt on Michigan's Upper Peninsula. Mike, Mitchell, and Ryan Stoychoff met him at the airport in Green Bay. They didn't mention the Packers, but they drove him twice around Lambeau Stadium before heading north to the U.P.

During the trip, Peabody learned the ruffed-grouse cycle was at its peak, Ryan's dog was behaving well and, in anticipation of the coming feed, Mike had brought shiitake mushrooms and bay leaves, both central to his woodstove grouse recipe.

They reached the Stoychoff camp late in the afternoon, and soon the van was unloaded and bunks were claimed. Later, with the fire going well and the cabin warm, a meal of wild mallard accompanied by a dusty French Bordeaux was comfortably beneath their belts as the four hunters made their plans.

Mitch suggested they hunt the edge of the slashing in the morning. Ryan thought the new growth of popple over by the clear-cut should hold some birds. Mike wanted to try the Section Nine creek bottom.

With the serious business concluded, the rest of the conversation was light and punctuated by laughter. By eleven they retired, smiling and thinking grousey thoughts. God was in his heaven, and all was right with the world. But their pleasant mood was in for a change.

After breakfast the next morning, Major Peabody and Mitch stood staring through the large window overlooking the Tamarack River. The stream was high, and they had a clear view of the white water bouncing down the rapids in front of the cabin. It was a beautiful scene. Neither man smiled. During the night, the first snow of the season had fallen. And the air had grown cold. And the wind had begun to blow.

Ryan, looking somewhat depressed, threw another chunk of wood on the fire, already blazing in the fieldstone fireplace that heated the log cabin. Then he joined the Major and Mitch, and helped them silently look out over the river. The thermometer, nailed to a hard maple growing near the window, showed the temperature had risen to thirty-nine degrees.

Mike, also depressed, swatted a few more of the flies that had regained consciousness in the warmth of the cabin, mistakenly thinking it must be spring and coming out of the many cracks in the walls to buzz the four hunters. Then he joined his companions at the window.

The boughs of the spruce and balsam trees outlining the river were bent down by the weight of the four-inch snowfall. A line from James Russell Lowell's *The First Snowfall* came to mind, and Mike quoted, "Every pine and fir and hemlock wore ermine too dear for an earl, and the poorest twig on the elm tree was ridged inch deep in pearl." But none of the three men smiled.

It was the snow that had raised the water level on the Tamarack and had given it its coursing beauty. And it was also the snow, abetted by the wind, that would keep the birds, with feathers fluffed out, obstinately sitting in the branches of the evergreens, refusing to move or come out to feed until more reasonable weather made its appearance.

And it was the snow and the wind that would make the four men cold, wet, and miserable if they made the questionable decision to leave the cabin and attempt their planned hunt for the ruffed grouse.

When Mike quoted Lowell, the Major gave him a questioning sideways glance. Peabody turned from the window and recalled what he considered to be the much more appropriate observation of Robert Burns, "The best laid schemes o' mice an' men gang aft aglee."

An overstuffed couch, discarded by someone's wife years ago, faced the fireplace. On either side of it, two large chairs—each showing stuffing—stood guard. Major Peabody sat in one of them and considered his situation. To suggest hunting in such weather would be the same as presenting a petition for a hearing before the Sanity Commission. And he wasn't in the mood for a four-man poker game. At that moment he felt any kind of card game would be about as welcome as a visitation by the black plague. It looked like a very dull, stale, and unprofitable day.

Perhaps the snow would melt and the birds would come out tomorrow. But perhaps it wouldn't, and even if it did, perhaps they wouldn't. The prospect of a three-day imprisonment in a cabin with the ruffed-grouse cycle at its peak was most unpleasant.

By now Mike, Mitch, and Ryan were seated, silently watching the fire. The three of them had consistently been on the wrong side of the Major's bets in the past. In fact, over the years they were never once successful. For the past twelve months, they had steadfastly refused to accept any of the wagers he had proposed. To be sure, the Major found such an attitude to be disagreeable. Then a thought occurred to him.

"Gentlemen," he said, "I will bet fifty dollars I can take my Lefever, leave this cabin, and come back in thirty minutes with a ruffed grouse."

Mike looked at Ryan, closed his eyes, and slowly nodded his head up and down. "I knew, sooner or later, it would come to this," he said.

"He's up to something, Ryan," said Mitch. "It's a sucker's bet. I know better than to take it. Anyone who takes it will lose. Just as surely as the sun rises in the morning, he'll lose."

Peabody merely smiled and looked at the fire. He knew their curiosity had been piqued. After a minute, Mike, not looking at him, questioned: "Dead or alive?"

"Dead, of course," answered the Major. After another few minutes, Ryan spoke up.

"Recently dead or dead for some time?" he asked. The Major thought for a minute and said, "The grouse I will bring into this cabin is, at present, very much alive."

While his companions pondered the proposition, searching for the loophole, Major Peabody smiled, said nothing, and watched the glowing coals. Mitch broke the silence. "Aha," he said, "I have it! You didn't say when you'd leave the cabin." With a triumphant grin he asked the Major, "Do you mean now, or at some future date—say, when the weather clears up or next fall?"

"Michael. Mitchell. Ryan." said the Major, affecting a wounded tone, "I'm surprised at the inferences made so obvious by your questioning. Do you suspect me capable of chicanery?" The three Stoychoffs exchanged looks, which clearly answered the question in the affirmative.

"I mean now," said the Major, "right now. In the midst of this blowing snow. Fifty dollars says I can leave this cabin, right now, and within a half hour be back with at least one recently shot ruffed grouse. I'll explain no further. The terms of the wager speak for themselves." And he sank back into the chair.

"Don't bite, Ryan," cautioned Mike. "I know him. And so do you. He's cost all of us goodly sums during the last ten years, and I don't intend to make any further contribution to his welfare." But he wondered what the Major had up his sleeve.

By noon it warmed up, the sun appeared, the wind died down, and the melting snow was falling from the trees. In spite of their coaxing and threats, Major Peabody would not divulge the deception that Mike, Mitch, and Ryan knew was hidden within his bet.

Later in the afternoon, they hunted with reasonable success. That evening, the Stoychoffs could stand it no longer. After a family conference, Mike approached the Major. "We have solemnly promised never to bet with you, Major," he announced, "but we have to know how you were going to pull this one off. We've chipped in ten dollars apiece. We'll give you thirty dollars if you'll tell us just what you were going to do."

Major Peabody nodded, took the three tens, carefully folded the bills, and pushed them into the pocket of his wool shirt. Then he smiled and said: "If you took my bet, I was going to lose. No one could get a bird in that weather."

173

31

THE COMPASS

MAJOR PEABODY ADVISED ME NEVER TO EAT woodcock. The flavor of the bird, he told me, was enhanced by soaking it in gasoline. He said he would eat woodcock if it were the only meat left on earth—but only under those circumstances.

We were at the Major's apartment, awaiting the stroke of midnight and the delivery of his monthly stipend. It was the thirtieth of September, the time to hunt woodcock was fast approaching, and Major Peabody was thinking of them. The woodcock, he informed me, prefer to frequent low lands—stream bottoms, tag alders, and the kind of moist territory where they can probe for worms with their long bills. He also admitted that, over the years, he had walked through, in, and around some very wild territory searching for them. The birds, not the worms.

My curiosity was aroused. I paused and looked directly at the Major until I had his attention and was sure he wouldn't miss the subtle nuance of my question. I asked him why anyone who claimed to maintain a semblance of mental equilibrium would slosh through brushy wetland to shoot at a bird that, apparently, no civilized person would eat. I emphasized the words "semblance of mental equilibrium."

Major Peabody caught the insult and snorted, but didn't say anything. So I continued. "From the way you describe the woodcock's habitat, it would seem to me that hunting the inedible bird represents only a good opportunity to become lost in a swamp."

The prospect of being disoriented in the woods terrifies me. And the Major knew it. On the few occasions when I found myself hunting with him, I dogged his steps and was never more than fifteen feet behind him. So Peabody gave only peremptory treatment to the first portion of my inquiry and moved directly to the matter in which my true interest lay—the fear of being lost in the wilderness.

"The most intelligent of our species," he said, looking directly at me to make sure I didn't miss the not-so-subtle nuance of his words, "respond to the natural urge to hunt that has been with mankind since before the time of *homo erectus*. Those individuals consider the prospect of an unbroken urban existence to be the equivalent of the torment suffered by the mythical Greek character whose liver was, each day, eaten by the buzzards.

"While you may find it strange, rational people prefer the solitude of the woods, broken only by game birds and hunting dogs. And, you may be sure, those hunters regularly lose their bearings. My boy," he said to me, "with one possible exception, you may be assured that anyone who doesn't admit to having been hopelessly lost on a number of occasions is treating the truth in a very cavalier manner—"

"You say, 'With one possible exception,' " I interrupted. "Just who might be that truthful and accomplished woodsman? Is it anyone I might know?" I fully expected Major Peabody to admit that he, himself, had never been lost in the woods. It remained an unfulfilled expectation.

"I'm not sure," he answered. "Do you know Radford Mueller? His friends call him 'Ratty.' "

"No," I answered, somewhat disappointed. I had looked forward to hearing some outrageous claim from the Major. "I don't know anyone named Radford 'Ratty' Mueller."

"A pity. You and Ratty have much in common. He's a Milwaukee stockbroker—a city-oriented fellow possessing little experience with either shotguns or nature's domain. I see him once a year at Steve Gress's annual International Woodcock Championship on Michigan's Upper Peninsula.

"Even though Ratty is no hunter, Steve thinks the world of him and insists that he always attend the tournament. It was Ratty who recommended a computer stock that went through the ceiling immediately after Steve bought it. Not only that. Ratty advised him to sell all of it just before the price reached its zenith, turned, and crashed back down to earth. Steve used some of the profits to buy a half section of land in the U. P. It's now the site of the woodcock hunt.

"Ratty, as I've already said, is a city type. The only time he leaves the environs of Milwaukee is when his wife hauls him to New York for shopping and culture. And—of course—when it's time for the annual visit to Steve's camp for the International Woodcock Championship. But Ratty enjoys a taste of camp life as well as the opportunity to maintain a close relationship with Steve, who is one of his good customers.

"Ratty is very careful to station himself near another hunter when he is in the woods, so his opportunity to become disoriented is limited. However, the rules of Steve's competition require each hunter to spend one day hunting alone.

"There are eight hunters and eight forty-acre parcels on Steve's land. We draw for the forties and spend one day hunting alone in our assigned area. Each of the competitors is given one box of shells. At the end of the hunt, the ratio between the hunter's woodcock body count and the shells he expended is calculated. The person with the smallest ratio has his name inscribed on a plaque, which hangs in a position of prominence on the cabin wall.

"During each of the first seven years of the championship, it was universally expected that we would have to search the woods for a lost Ratty. But he hunted strange country in all of those seven annual events and never became lost.

"Ratty's secret is his compass, which he bought in a Milwaukee pawnshop. It is very old and very big—I'd say between six and seven inches in diameter. I believe it must have once belonged to a Great Lakes sailing ship captain. It is made of brass, and Ratty keeps it highly polished.

"His expert use of that compass came to light last year. Steve knew Ratty had a hard time finding the cabin outhouse so he finally asked his friend how come he never got lost in the woods.

"Ratty reached into his wool coat pocket and pulled out that big brass compass. 'It's easy when you have an instrument like this,' he said. 'I drive to the forty I've been assigned, park the car, and walk into the woods. When I'm in so deep I can just see the car, I take out this compass and hang it on a tree. Then I hunt,' he concluded.

"When mild disbelief and wonderment were expressed by his campmates, Ratty added, 'Oh, I never hunt so far away from this big shiny compass that I can't see it.'

"Yes," said the Major, "even in the hands of a neophyte, a compass is a handy tool."

32

IT'S THE PRINCIPLE
OF THE THING

AFTER HE WAS APPROPRIATELY PROVISIONED with a refill of my single-malt scotch and one of the twenty-five H. Upmann cigars he had given me for Christmas, the Major sank into my favorite overstuffed chair sipped, lit up, blew a smoke ring, and sipped again.

He then said: "Principles are important in a man's life. The dictionary tells us the word means a moral, political, or other rule, tenet, or conviction that serves as a guide for conduct or action. To claim a man is without principles is, indeed, a very serious charge. It accuses him of having not a single rule to govern either his own life or his relations with his fellow man.

"We may not agree with a particular conviction a man may have adopted. We may even find it to be reprehensible. But, usually a man has at least one principle. For example, look at the politicians. They are widely denounced as being without principles. And, granted, any firm and steadfast principle a politician proclaims, you may be assured, will, at best, have a half-life of only about four months.

"But these people are not entirely unprincipled. Any and all of them will say and do anything in order to get reelected and avoid honest labor. That is the one and only immutable principle they all share.

"While the politician may have only one principle, on the opposite end of the spectrum there are others who claim to have adopted all principles that are alleged to be righteous and to enjoy the full support of all known deities and right-thinking men.

"Eliminating from this second group those who publicly proclaim a variety of pleasant-sounding ethical standards but, in private life, regularly disregard them, we find only a few people who are truly, indiscriminately multiprincipled.

"A man who chooses to stand between the two extremes of the single-principled and the multiprincipled can adopt a number of alternative rules. The selection of one's principles is a serious business not to be lightly undertaken.

"We are told to 'Look before you leap.' That's a good rule. But 'He who hesitates is lost' is equally good. Suppose you find yourself somewhere in the Maine woods running from a huge, short-tempered black bear, and suppose this bear chases you up a very high bank that ends abruptly, looking way down upon a fast-moving, boulder-strewn river. As the bear approaches, you will have to make a very important decision about which of these two principles will determine your conduct.

"The axiom 'Do unto others as you would have them do unto you' is another good principle. But if you have thoughtlessly adopted it and attempt to apply it while playing seven-card stud, you will have no occasion to report gambling winnings on your federal income tax return. In such circumstances, the more prudent man will adopt a different principle. I refer, of course, to 'Never give a sucker an even break.'

"My point is," said the Major, "the selection of the principles that will govern a man's life is an important occupation requiring both foresight and skill.

"You are going to tell me you have principles?" I ventured.

"I'll ignore your tone of voice," he said. "Of course I have principles. I have adopted rigid rules to govern my conduct. Let me give you an example.

"It was in northern Wisconsin. It was in December. It was cold. Very cold. So cold that there will be no next generation produced by the brass monkeys inhabiting that part of the country. Though I am said to assign a high priority to shotgunning and allied interests, it is against my principles to look for ruffed grouse when the temperature is below zero."

The Major paused for a second and then added a qualification. "I mean Fahrenheit. Zero degrees on the Celsius scale is not so bad if the hunting is good.

"Well, it was twenty-three degrees below—Fahrenheit. The radio weatherman claimed the wind was coming from the northwest at twenty miles per hour. The wind-chill factor was minus seventy-three degrees, and I didn't feel any better when he advised us that this was only sixty-eight degrees below zero on the Celsius scale.

"Our log cabin was heated by a large stone fireplace. It wasn't particularly efficient and used a lot of oxygen to burn the logs. The necessary air was cleverly provided by the design of the cabin. You could see daylight through the cracks around the door and, in a few places, between the logs that formed the walls. The wind swept through them and up the chimney.

"The cabin's design had another advantage. If food and beverages (with less than 120-proof alcohol content) were placed outside, by morning they would all be frozen. If they were stored inside the cabin, they would not freeze solid but would stay colder than the minimum temperature required for the growth of bacteria.

"Five face cord of oak and beech were stacked in the snow near the kitchen door. Little of it was split. Early in my youth, I discovered that the handles on both the two-faced ax and the splitting wedge did not comfortably fit my hand. Still, I happily took my turn chopping large chunks of tree into smaller pieces and kindling for the kitchen woodstove. It has been accurately stated, 'Split your own wood, and it will warm you twice.'

We didn't hunt. We stayed inside the cabin and often threw wood on the fire. It still took three hours before we could no longer see our breath. The floor, the walls, and the furniture warmed more slowly. After a few more hours, the heat flowed into my fingers, and it was no longer difficult to deal the cards.

"When it came time to turn in, I claimed the couch and let my companions take the more comfortable bunks at the far end of the building, near the drafty door. After I pulled the couch close to the fireplace, I slept like a top.

"By that I mean I spun around throughout the night. By the time the side of me that was closest to the fire got toasty warm, the part pointed in the opposite direction was frigid. By turning over, my cold backside would face the fire. But as it warmed up, the other side took its turn to freeze. I was almost constantly in motion.

"When the sun finally arose, I lit a fire in the woodstove and prepared a hearty breakfast of sausages, raw fried potatoes, toast, marmalade, and coffee—lots of coffee. I thought the meal would do the trick and, of course, ate quite sparingly myself. This scenario was repeated every morning and produced the desired results during each of the five days we were holed up in that cabin."

Desired results? I thought perhaps I had missed part of the story. "What desired results?" I questioned.

"This was not a modern building," the Major explained. "By that I mean it did not have running water. By that I mean there was an outhouse. The quality and the quantity of the breakfasts were calculated to jump-start the digestive processes of my companions and necessitate their early visit to said outbuilding.

"My boy, it is a direct violation of one of my most sacred principles to be the first one to warm the seat of an outhouse when it has been exposed to a temperature of twenty-three degrees below zero."

33

THE MAJOR TAKES A HOLIDAY

"ALL WORK AND NO PLAY MAKES JACK A DULL BOY," I said to Major Nathaniel Peabody as he sat in my apartment on the evening of the last day of the month, awaiting midnight and the delivery of his monthly check.

"Oh?" questioned the Major as he tilted his head a bit to the left, lowered his chin, narrowed his eyes somewhat, and kept them on me. "And just what do you mean by that, young man?"

I'll admit I had an ulterior motive. If I could get the Major away from his hunting gang and, perhaps, get him accustomed to visiting sportsman's shows, he'd be involved in a less expensive pastime and, maybe—just maybe—he'd get to the end of the month without being broke (and prodding me for a never-to-be-repaid subsidy).

Previous association with Major Nathaniel Peabody had taught me the advantages of misdirection and duplicity. So, I answered his question as follows: "Major, you get your monthly checks and, without exception or variation, immediately go off on some bird-hunting expedition."

"Not so," said the Major. "I've gone to some very interesting gun-dog trials and sporting-clay events."

"You know very well what I'm saying," I continued. "There is more to life than firing a shotgun over a dog." The Major didn't answer, and a quizzical look came over his face—as if he had bitten into a lime. "Instead of your next hunt in God knows where, why don't you go to New York and spend a week there? Take in the sportsman's show at the Madison Square Garden. See what's new in both hunting and fishing. Stay with your cousin, Maude. You'd enjoy it."

"You don't know my Cousin Maudie," he said. "She's a lot like Great-Aunt Aurora—in a word, 'insufferable.' And, you will remember, she is one of the contingent beneficiaries of my spendthrift trust. When I die she stands to get a bundle. I wouldn't think of visiting her. If she ever got the chance, she'd put poison in my soup."

"Then go to a hotel. I'll sponsor two nights at the Hotel Astor."

And so it came to pass. Major Peabody would go to New York City. I didn't know that his decision was based on his recollection that guides and outfitters maintained booths at sports shows. He thought he might be able to find a new place to hunt.

On Monday morning, six days later, my phone rang. It was the Major. He was at the railroad station and insisted I meet him there at my "absolutely earliest convenience." There was a sense of urgency in his voice, and I knew something was up.

The Major was seated alone on a bench. He looked awful. He was pale. He was unshaven. His shoulders stooped. When he saw me, he seemed genuinely pleased.

"I need lunch desperately," were his first words. The ride to the restaurant wasn't productive insofar as conversation was concerned. Responses to my questions were largely single syllabled.

"How was your weekend?"

"Terrible."

(Pause)

"You look a bit peaked. How do you feel?"

"Terrible."

(Pause)

"Did you enjoy New York City?"

"No."

(Pause)

"Well, we'll talk about it at lunch."

"I suppose."

After he took aboard chicken cordon bleu and a scotch and water, the Major's color came back and he recounted his weekend experience. It had been a disaster.

The Major arrived at the Pennsylvania Station in New York on Friday. As he left the train and passed a group of four men huddled together, he heard his second language, Spanish, being spoken. The men were obviously strangers in a foreign land. So he stopped to volunteer assistance.

Having a free hand (the Major travels light), he picked up one of their bags and as he walked them toward the taxi stands, he inquired whether they had made hotel reservations. They had not. The discussion of accommodations continued until the group left the station.

A few steps later, they all found themselves confronted by people with guns. It happened quickly, and the Major admitted, "When faced with someone leveling a firearm at my head, I follow directions very quickly and very carefully."

"Since all this happened in broad daylight, I expected representatives of the New York City Police Department to appear. I looked for a place to hide when the shooting began.

"Fortunately, there was no shooting. Unfortunately, it *was* the police who were pointing the weapons at me. They spread-eagled me on the hood of the police car. They frisked me, touching me where no member of my own sex had ever before touched me. They extended me the courtesy of putting a hand over my head to protect it as they shoved me into the vehicle.

"Now, young man," the Major said to me, "I have a well-developed sense of humor and enjoy telling a good story, but I don't consider any of the following statements to be as funny as the police did:

1. 'You have made a terrible mistake.' (Laughter)

2. 'I am not with these people.' (Laughter)

3. 'I'm a retired United States Army major on my way to a New York City sports show.' (Laughter)

"The only comments made by the police were:

1. 'Why were you carrying a bag containing three kilos of raw cocaine?'

2. 'You have the right to remain silent. Anything you say may be . . .' etc., etc.

"I placed my one phone call to Freddie Beyer, a stockbroker and quail-shooting companion. His maid, in a heavy accent—I believe it was central European, probably Bulgarian—said he was hunting in Virginia and wouldn't be back for a week. She said she'd give him the message. Then she hung up before I could say anything else.

"I won't bore you with a full report of the pleasantries occasioned by being booked, fingerprinted, interrogated, and put in a cell with criminals more frightening than any I've seen since visiting the United States Senate.

"After three days of enjoying those accommodations, yesterday evening they took me from the cell. I was prepared to say: 'No blindfold, please. Let me smoke one last cigar and then fire.' It was my intention to ask for a Churchill—the biggest cigar I could remember.

"However, I was given my wallet, watch, belt, and shoelaces and was told that the police department's investigation had shown that the drug-enforcement people were looking for only four Colombians, that I was what I purported to be, and that they had no reason to connect me with the drug ring.

"The experience so moved me that I elected to get out of New York City as fast as possible. I taxied back to the railroad station and purchased my return ticket to Philadelphia. Then I waited for the late train.

"I made the mistake of visiting the bathroom, where I met a delightful man armed with a .357 magnum revolver. He relieved me of my watch, suitcase, and wallet. After convincingly promising to blow my head off if I stuck it into the waiting room within the next sixty minutes, he took his leave.

"So much for the Sullivan law, passed in the 1930s to protect New Yorkers from handgun crimes. Though I am a shotgun man, as soon as my treasury is in proper order, I will join the National Rifle Association.

"And that brings me to my next point. It was you, my young friend, who convinced me to go to New York instead of taking a hunting trip. You not only exposed me to substantial danger, but additionally, you are the reason I am bereft of watch, suitcase, and wardrobe, and have not so much as a single Mexican *centavo* in my pocket. As you are fully aware, I have another twenty-four days to go before the delivery of my next remittance."

Then he was silent and merely stared at me.

I should never try to correct Major Peabody's wayward ways. Whenever I do, I get on the wrong side of the Gods of Shotgunning, and they punish me. The result of this latest misguided effort was a $2,500 "loan."

My chance of recovering any part of that loan is only slightly better than the chance that Pluto will suddenly fly out of its orbit and collide with Venus.

34

THE GOOD LIFE
OF NATHANIEL PEABODY

SOME PEOPLE HAVE GOOD HEALTH. They jog and watch their diet and take vitamins. Some of them work out—on a beach or inside a gym. I don't go to a gym, but I believe it is important to exercise regularly. In the morning, before breakfast, it is my usual practice to don a sweatsuit and run the three-mile course I measured out from my apartment door.

The condition of Major Peabody's health concerns me. He shows no outward sign of deterioration, but I'm sure he would be healthier and happier if he would exercise. The Major, however, opposes such a suggestion. He considers exercise to be work, and he doesn't enjoy work. When I explained my jogging program to him, he questioned me: "How can you possibly enjoy good health if you have to work at it?"

"It's good for me," I argued. "I'll live longer."

Peabody lit another Dominican Republic cigar and answered, "Oh? Are you sure? Your jogging unnecessarily exposes you to life-threatening dangers. You might be hit by a car as you run down the street. You might be mugged running alone and unarmed in a city park. The police may see you running, presume you've committed some heinous crime, and—as is their custom—shoot you dead without warning."

The best I could do in way of defense was, "Oh, come now, Major."

Peabody blew a cloud of smoke into the air. "If you manage to evade those forms of early death, I suppose you might be able to add a few years to the time given you by the mortality tables, but I wonder—is the game worth the candle? I doubt it." The Major took a pencil and pad from the table beside him and continued.

"Let's say it takes you an hour-and-a-half to perform your despicable act of jogging. That would include preparation time, running time, and the time you spend leaning against the side of your apartment building gasping for breath when you've finished the three-mile course.

"One-and-a-half hours per day—365 days per year—for thirty years . . . " he murmured as he performed some calculations. He looked at the results, nodded, and said, to himself, "I'll have to add a bit to take into account the leap years and the extra distances you'll run because of the times you've been chased by vicious dogs."

After a few more notations, he said, "There you have it, my boy." The Major handed me the pad. "Study it. The conclusion is inescapable. You'll spend about two years of your life jogging. That's about equal to the few years all that running will have added to your life expectancy. It looks like a wash to me. And, besides, you'll probably spend those extra two years of your life strapped to a wheelchair in some nursing home."

What can you do with a man like that? I thought. He could buy a stationary bicycle or a home treadmill, but he won't. He'll spend his money on trips to Canada or Argentina or North Dakota or Wisconsin, frittering away his time chasing a dog that's following running pheasants—or plowing through thick undergrowth looking for ruffed grouse—or walking miles just to build a blind and shoot at geese.

I do wish he'd get more exercise.

As long as I'm complaining about the Major, I'll tell you something else. He doesn't visit the doctor for an annual checkup. I'm many years his junior, and I go twice a year. He hunts with Doctor Carmichael. It wouldn't be hard to drop into his office from time to time. I've often tried to get him to make an appointment for a general physical. Those attempts have all been unsuccessful.

On this particular evening, we'd returned to my apartment for a nightcap after a dinner at Bookbinders. We were talking about health.

"Young man," he said, "if you are to lead a long, happy and healthy life, there are three rules you must follow. First, you must assiduously avoid funeral directors. If you can push off dealing with them for eighty years or more, you will have had a long life.

"Second, to ensure your happiness, you must avoid lawyers." The Major noticed that I winced. "Let me be clear," he said, "If you will recall the aphorism, 'Lie down with dogs, get up with fleas,' you will never be tempted to associate with any lawyer who has abandoned the practice in favor of politics. Regarding the rest, if you are to be happy, avoid all professional association with them, too. Remember the Italian proverb, 'A rat in the jaws of a cat is better off than a client in the hands of an attorney."

I winced again, and the Major noticed again. "On a selective basis, however," he conceded in deference to me, "it's all right to have social dealings with them. In the field and in camp, they tend to be pleasant companions."

I felt much better.

Then he added, "They are especially welcome at the poker table, where they have—very often—contributed to my happiness." I winced again.

"As far as good health is concerned," he said, "the final rule is, 'To maintain a sound body, never use the services of the medical profession.' "

There was a reason behind starting the conversation of health and exercise. I wanted Major Peabody to go to his friend, Doctor Carmichael, for a physical examination. Now, after his more than somewhat cynical statements, I knew my task would not be easy, but I didn't give up. Maybe I could appeal to Peabody's manhood.

"Major," I said, "you can't really believe that. You aren't afraid of a visit to a doctor's office, are you? Is that it? Are you afraid of doctors?"

"Of course I'm afraid of doctors," he answered. "Any sane person is afraid of them. How many times have you seen someone go to a *medico* with some common complaint—like chest pains. The doctor give the man some pills and scares the hell out of him. It doesn't take long before the poor guy dies of a heart attack."

"I've noticed," he went on, "that doctors never misdiagnose an ailment. If a doctor says you've got measles, the death certificate will say measles was the cause of your death. Never mind the rumor that you had malaria." The Major paused and contemplated the coal on the end of his cigar. "Of course," he said, "it is always the doctor who fills out the death certificate."

I decided to openly raise the question of his medical exam. "Major Peabody," I said, "isn't it about time you went to see Doctor Carmichael for a checkup?" He just looked at me. I continued, "When was the last time you went to a doctor?"

"For your information, young man, it was nine months ago. Doc Carmichael said I had a particularly virulent, but then latent, form of pneumonia. In his report, he described me as a carrier— kind of a Typhoid Mary."

This was, indeed, disturbing news, and I asked about the current state of his health.

"Nothing to worry about. I am in perfect health, and I was in perfect health then, too. You see, it was the first week of the duck season. After the judge read Carmichael's medical report, he excused me from jury duty, and the Doc and I were able to go to Maryland for the opening day of the hunting season.

I know when I'm beaten. I gave up.